On the Road

Tourism English for Travelers 2

Andrew Crosthwaite

CENGAGE

Australia • Brazil • Canada • Mexico • Singapore • United Kingdom • United States

CENGAGE

On the Road 2
Tourism English for Travelers
Andrew Crosthwaite

Senior Regional Director, Greater China & Asia Marketing :
Michael Cahill

Publisher, Asia ELT:
Edward Yoshioka

Assistant Manager, Publishing:
Melody Chiu

Editor:
Percy Chang

Senior Production Executive:
Evan Wu

Compositor:
Cynthia Chou

ISBN: 978-4-86312-401-1

Cengage Learning K.K.
No. 2 Funato Building, 5F
1-11-11 Kudankita, Chiyoda-ku
Tokyo 102-0073, Japan

Cengage Learning is a leading provider of customized learning solutions with office locations around the globe, including Singapore, the United Kingdom, Australia, Mexico, Brazil, and Japan.

Locate your local office at **www.cengage.com**

To learn more about Cengage Learning Solutions, visit **www.cengageasia.com**

Printed in Taiwan
Print Number: 01 Print Year: 2022

On the Road

Tourism English for Travelers

If you've ever been lost for words while traveling to another country, the *On the Road* series could be the books for you. There are two books, which are aimed at elementary and pre-intermediate level students. The overall aim of the series is to give English learners the basic tools they'll need to effectively communicate in English on their vacations.

Each *On the Road* book contains 15 teaching units, and they've been carefully designed to cover everything you need to know, from booking your trip to ordering room service to buying souvenirs. The units are grouped into five similarly themed sections. At the end of each section, there's a review unit with listening and reading questions to ensure smooth progress through the book.

The *On the Road* series deals with all four skills: reading, writing, speaking, and listening. There are two dialogues in each unit for you to listen to. They deal with real-life situations and introduce helpful new words and phrases that should make life easier for you when traveling overseas. There are reading comprehension passages with questions that target both major themes and specific pieces of information. A different grammar point is covered in each unit, and you'll have the chance to practice using them in the writing section. There are also lots of opportunities to speak, as each unit begins with a simple speaking exercise and finishes with two more in-depth activities.

While the central aim of these books is to help learners deal with overseas travel situations comfortably and confidently, the *On the Road* series provides a strong foundation in English for all students, no matter how often they want to take vacations.

For vacation English and a great, all-round learning experience, you should pick up this series of books and pack it up every time you're *On the Road*!

Table of Contents

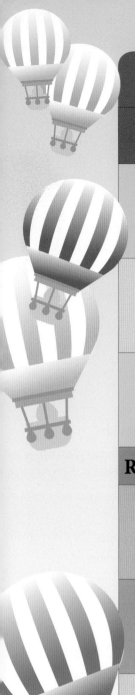

Unit 1

Trip of a Lifetime

By the end of this unit, you will be able to do the following:

- Discuss travel plans
- Talk about guided tours and activities
- Compare tour features
- Ask for and give opinions

Before We Go

There are many different kinds of vacations you can go on to see the world. Look at the following pictures of different trips. Use the vacation terms in the box to label each picture.

adventure trip	*bicycle tour*	*cruise*	*cultural tour*
ecotourism	*food tour*	*luxury trip*	*volunteer vacation*

❶ ______ ❷ ______ ❸ ______ ❹ ______

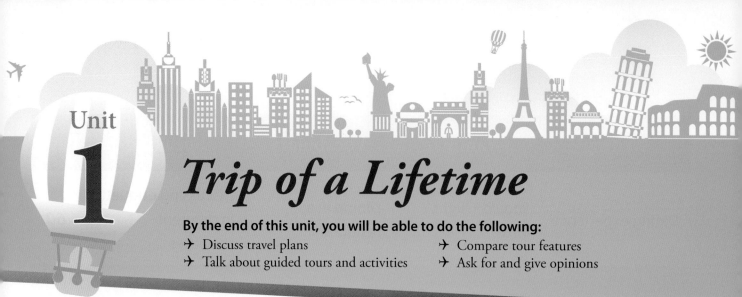

❺ ______ ❻ ______ ❼ ______ ❽ ______

Useful Expressions

- I would most like to go on *a cruise* because *I enjoy the service.*
- I don't think that I would ever want to try *bicycle trip*.
- That kind of trip allows you to *have fun, help others, and make friends.*
- I know someone who went on *a safari*. He/She thought it was *exciting*.

Conversation 1

Track 2 Robert visits a travel agent to talk about his options for a month-long European vacation. Listen to the conversation and fill in the missing words.

Robert: Can you tell me a little about the differences between Dream Tours and All-Europe Tours?

Agent: Of course. With Dream Tours, you'll stay in ❶ ______ hotels, eat at ❷ ______ restaurants, and travel in ❸ ______ ❹ ______ all the way.

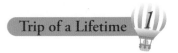

Robert: I think I would really like that.

Agent: Well, All-Europe Tours offers luxury ❺ ______, traveling, and ❻ ______ options, too.

Robert: So, what are the differences?

Agent: The ❼ ______ for Dream Tours is a little more ❽ ______. If you chose Dream Tours, you would visit five countries in one month and have time in each country to explore on your own.

Robert: There's nothing wrong with that! What does All-Europe Tours offer?

Agent: Well, if you went with them, you would see ten different countries in the same time frame.

Robert: I see. That's a hard choice. If I picked Dream Tours, I would get to experience more in each place we visited. If I chose All-Europe Tours, I would see more countries, but I would feel more ❾ ______.

Agent: I have clients who have gone on these tours before. If you wanted, I could put you in touch with them, and you could get a better idea of what each experience would be like.

Robert: I'd like that a lot. Thanks.

Words to Remember

Use the words in the box to complete the sentences.

itinerary	*four-star*	*dining*	*travel agent*	*luxury*
first-class	*rushed*	*accommodation*	*laid-back*	*gourmet*

1. If you like ______ food, you should go to Nielson's. It's the best restaurant in the city.
2. I want to arrive at the airport early. That way, I won't feel ______ while checking in.
3. I never use ______. I always book vacations on my own.
4. My friend Steve is very ______. He never worries about anything.
5. The seats in the economy section are always cramped. There's a lot more room in the ______ section.

Reading

Track 3 **Robert has researched both trips a little more but is still having difficulty deciding which tour to choose. Read the following pros and cons lists that he has written for the tours.**

DREAM TOURS

Pros: If I took this tour, I would enjoy a luxurious vacation as I slowly moved through Europe.

If I wanted to have time to do my own things when I went to a particular city, I would be able to.

I would spend a longer amount of time in each country. If I did that, I would start to feel more like a local and less like a tourist.

I would feel more relaxed if I went on this trip because it would be more laid-back.

Cons: I would see only five countries if I took part in this tour.

If I picked Dream Tours, I wouldn't get to stay in a castle in Germany.

ALL-EUROPE TOURS

Pros: If I took this tour, I would travel in a very luxurious style.

I would visit ten countries if I selected this tour company.

If I went on this trip, I would stay in a castle in Germany for two nights!

I would feel that I had seen everything I could if I followed this trip's itinerary.

Cons: If I did everything this trip offers, I would feel pretty rushed.

There's a chance that I wouldn't get to see as much in each country as I would see if I chose Dream Tours.

If I didn't make myself rest on this trip, I would return from it feeling exhausted!

Give It a Try

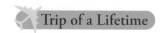

Based on the list, choose the correct answers for the following questions.

1. Which of the following is a pro of choosing Dream Tours?
   a. Robert would have more time for himself.
   b. Robert would travel more luxuriously.
   c. Robert could spend more time in the cities he likes.
   d. Robert would be able to travel on his own.
2. How would Robert feel if he could spend more time in each country?
   a. More interested in the vacation
   b. More relaxed with the tourists
   c. More like a local resident
   d. More friendly to the locals
3. What special place could Robert stay in if he chose All-Europe Tours?
   a. An old hostel
   b. A German guesthouse
   c. A luxurious hotel
   d. A castle
4. Which of the following is a pro choosing All-Europe Tours?
   a. Robert would feel he had seen everything he could.
   b. Robert would not end up feeling rushed.
   c. Robert could choose what countries he visited.
   d. Robert would travel in luxury buses.
5. If Robert chose All-Europe Tours, what would he have to do to avoid feeling exhausted?
   a. Go to bed early.
   b. Get lots of rest.
   c. Not follow the itinerary.
   d. Go home early.

Conversation 2

Track 4 The travel agent put Robert in contact with Evelyn, a woman who has traveled with Dream Tours before. Listen to the conversation and fill in the missing words.

Robert: Thanks for taking the time to talk with me about your tour experience.

Evelyn: It's my pleasure. I highly ❶ ________ signing up for one.

Robert: Really? It was that great?

Evelyn: Definitely. There were so many activities on the itinerary, and they even ❷ ________ ❸ ________ to us for our free time.

Robert: What kinds of things did they suggest that you do?

Evelyn: Well, in Italy, I had a whole day free. The guide suggested that I should rent a car and drive to a nearby ❹ ________. She even arranged for a ❺ ________ lunch.

Robert: Weren't you nervous about the car ❻ ________? The ❼ ________ in Italy is supposed to be crazy!

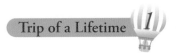

Evelyn: It wasn't that bad. You should get your ❽ ________ before you go, just in case.

Robert: We'll see about that. What other suggestions do you have?

Evelyn: There is an option to ❾ ________ your trip by four days. It's more expensive, but I suggest doing it. On the longer trip, you get to take a river cruise. It was definitely worth it.

Robert: You've given me a lot to think about. Thanks for your suggestions!

Words to Remember

Use the words in the box to complete the sentences.

recommend	*extend*	*picnic*	*rental*	*international driver's license*
suggest	*villa*	*traffic*	*outing*	

1. If the weather's nice tomorrow, we can take some food to the park and have a ________.
2. If you go to Paris, I would ________ going to see the Eiffel Tower.
3. This isn't my car. It's just a ________ I picked up for the day.
4. I ________ that you go to the hospital to have that cut looked at.
5. Your membership at the club runs out next week, but you can ________ it for $15.

Get It Right

A. Scan the following example of a travel brochure for Portland to familiarize yourself with the writing style.

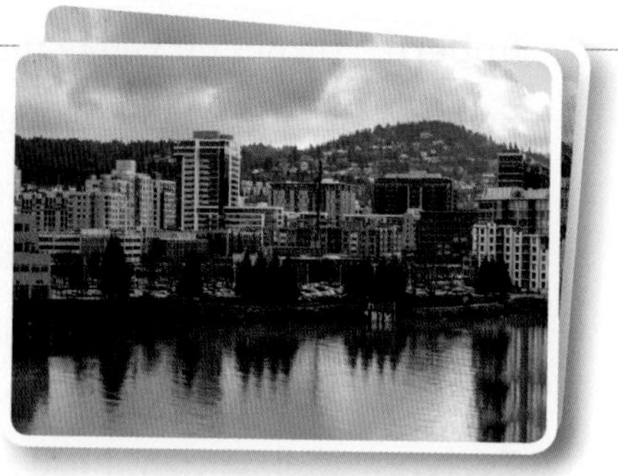

Welcome to Portland, Oregon! This beautiful town, known as the Rose City, lies in the northwest of the U.S. We recommend that you start off your trip by exploring downtown, where you will find interesting museums, unique shops, and the best restaurants. There's plenty to do here, so you should leave lots of time to explore. We also recommend heading to the coast to go sightseeing in cute beach towns and try water activities, like sailing or sea kayaking. When you get hungry, we suggest the local seafood as a perfect, delicious meal. Finally, any Portlander would suggest that you should visit the nearby mountains. Whether you choose to hike, ski, or simply drive through, their beauty will amaze you.

B. Now imagine you are writing a travel brochure for your country or hometown. What would you suggest that people see or do? Refer to the Grammar Bite for help.

Grammar Bite

You can use several different structures to make suggestions.

A. Recommend & suggest

1. recommend / suggest (that) sb. + V. • What did they *suggest* that you do? **2. recommend / suggest + N.** • They *suggested* outings.	**3. recommend / suggest + V-ing** • I *recommend* signing up for it. **4. suggest that sb. + V.** • The guide *suggested* that I rent a car.

B. Should

1. should + V.

- You *should* get your international driver's license before you go.

Give It a Try

Respond to each situation with a suggestion from the box. Use a different structure for each answer.

study harder	***fruit***	***see a doctor***

1. I'm hungry, but I don't know what to eat.

I recommend that you eat fruit.

2. I want to pass the math test.

____

3. I hurt my arm when I was playing basketball.

____

Prepare Yourself

Look at the two travel brochures below. Look up any words that you don't know.

See Europe in STYLE!

This popular trip starts with luxury in Rome and ends with five-star treatment in London. You will also stop in Florence, Lucerne, Nice, and Paris.

All the "must-see" features (Rome's Colosseum , Florence's finest museums, St. Mark's Basilica, the Eiffel Tower, and the British Museum) are included.

Learn how to make pasta by hand in Italy, travel by train through the Swiss Alps, enjoy a night at the theater in London, and lounge on the beaches of southern France.

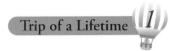

Hawaii Life Tours

On the Big Island of Hawaii, you'll visit one of the world's most active volcanoes, travel by bike along beautiful costal roads, experience ocean kayaking, and ride horses on the beach.

What's even better is that this action-packed vacation is environmentally friendly! You'll stay in eco-lodges around the island, eat locally grown organic food, and visit plant and animal conservation areas. There's even a one-day eco-cruise.

Don't worry—we've also scheduled plenty of free time in which you can choose from further eco-adventures or simply relax on the beach.

Activity 1

With a partner, discuss the two trips advertised in the brochures above. Which trip appeals to you more? Why?

Activity 2

Imagine that you are a travel agent and the three people below come into your office to book a tour. Based on their likes and dislikes, select the best tour for each person. Then, compare your answers with your classmates and explain your reasons for your recommendations.

Angela likes...	**Mark likes...**	**Julie likes...**
beaches	cities	being eco-friendly
cruises	going to museums	the outdoors
relaxing vacations	luxury vacations	adventure trips

Useful Expressions

- I like See Europe in STYLE because it offers *a theater trip*.
- I think Hawaii Life Tours would be the best trip because it offers *luxury vacations*.
- I would recommend that trip to *Mark* because he likes *cities*, and he can visit them on that trip.

Unit 2

How Much Should I Bring?

By the end of this unit, you will be able to do the following:

- Have a conversation about what you need for different vacations
- Plan your money for a vacation
- Talk about future situations
- Give advice on how to pack for a vacation

Before We Go

Depending on where you go on vacation, deciding what to take with you can be either difficult or almost impossible. Look at the picture of vacation essentials below, and use the words from the box to correctly label each item.

sun cream	*guide book*	*swimsuit*	*sunglasses*
toiletry bag	*passport*	*foreign currency*	*credit card*

① ______

② ______

③ ______

④ ______

⑤ ______

⑥ ______

⑦ ______

⑧ ______

Useful Expressions

- I always pack a *guide book* when I go on vacation because *they're very helpful.*
- I rarely take a *credit card*; I don't think they're important.
- I think *toiletry bags* are essential because *you always want to be clean and fresh.*
- The first thing I think of when packing is my *passport*.

Conversation 1

Track 5 Stacey is going on vacation to Thailand but is unsure about how much of the local currency she should take with her. She calls her travel agent to ask for advice. Listen to the conversation and fill in the missing words.

Stacey: I'm going to the bank later to exchange some money for Thai Baht, but I'm not really sure how much I should get. What do you think?

Agent: I wouldn't change very much money if I were you. It's ❶ ______ to carry around too much ❷ ______, especially when you're a tourist in a foreign country.

Stacey: That makes sense. So what should I do for spending money?

Agent: Well, a lot of people now use credit cards because they're convenient and the ❸ ______ you get with them are very good.

Stacey: Unfortunately, I don't have one.

Agent: In that case, you could take ❹ ______.

Stacey: Don't you have to pay a ❺ ______ for them?

Agent: Generally not if you get them from your usual bank, but either way, traveler's checks can be replaced if they're lost or stolen. Most tourists enjoy having that kind of ❻ ______.

Stacey: I think I would, too. So how much do you think I should get? I'd like to take some trips while I'm in the country, but I'm not interested in buying ❼ ______ gifts or ❽ ______; I'll get my food from street ❾ ______.

Agent: You should still take more than you think you need. You don't want to run out of money and have to start budgeting halfway through your vacation.

Stacey: Yeah, OK. I guess I can always ❿ ______ my traveler's checks when I get home.

Agent: Exactly.

Words to Remember

Use the words in the box to complete the sentences.

risky	*cash*	*exchange rate*	*traveler's check*	*commission*
guarantee	*fancy*	*fine-dining*	*vendor*	*redeem*

1. Every time the actor gets paid, 10% of the money goes to his manager as ______.
2. I never carry very much ______ as I generally pay for things by credit card.
3. I don't really like ______ clothes. I prefer things that are quite simple.
4. You can ______ this money-off coupon at your local supermarket.
5. This TV came with a two-year ______ so I can have it fixed if it breaks.

Reading

Track 6 **After talking to her travel agent, Stacey decides to do some more research on how to get money for her vacation. Read the tips given on this Web site.**

Travelview.com

How to manage your vacation money

There are many different ways you can change money into the local currency when you go on vacation. They all have their own strengths and weaknesses.

- **Changing money at the airport or your hotel**

  This is a very convenient way to get your hands on local currency, but you might end up paying for that convenience in other ways. Exchange rates at airport foreign exchange desks are generally good, but some companies will charge you a lot in service costs. Exchange rates in hotels are usually poor, and there are sometimes service charges as well.

- **Taking traveler's checks**

  This is probably the safest way to get your money as lost or stolen traveler's checks can be replaced for free. Changing your traveler's checks can take a long time, though, and often involves queuing for a long time in a local bank.

- **Using a credit card**

  Credit cards are now very popular as the exchange rates you can get with them are mostly very good. They're easy to use and very convenient. The only possible problem is that if you lose your credit card, you could be in trouble.

- **Using an ATM card**

  Getting your money from an ATM is really easy, and the exchange rates you can get with ATM cards is fairly good. The only problem is that the ATMs in some remote locations may not accept ATM cards from other countries. If you're going somewhere unusual, do some research before you set off.

Give It a Try

Based on the tips, choose the correct answers for the following questions.

1. With which method will you likely get the worst exchange rate?
   a. Using traveler's checks
   b. Changing money at the airport
   c. Changing money at your hotel
   d. Using a credit card
2. What are you advised to research if you plan to use an ATM card?
   a. Whether ATMs at your destination accept foreign cards.
   b. Whether there are any ATMs at your vacation destination.
   c. How much your bank charges in service costs.
   d. What the best ATM card to use is.
3. What is the slowest method for exchanging money?
   a. Credit cards
   b. Traveler's checks
   c. An airport cash transfer
   d. ATM cards
4. Why might foreign exchange desks at airports not be a good choice?
   a. There are sometimes high extra charges.
   b. They can be difficult to find.
   c. The exchange rates are not good.
   d. They are often inconvenient to use.
5. Which method should you use if you often lose things?
   a. ATM cards
   b. Credit cards
   c. Cash transfers
   d. Traveler's checks

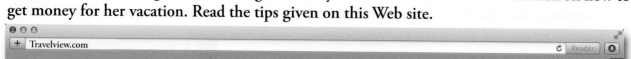

Conversation 2

Track 7 Stacey is having trouble packing and can't fit everything she wants to take into her luggage. She asks her brother, Mike, for help. Listen to the conversation and fill in the missing words.

Stacey: I don't know what I'm going to do. I've tried packing this bag three times already, but I can't ❶ ______ everything in.

Mike: You do seem to be taking a lot. Are you sure you need all of that?

Stacey: I just want to be ready for any ❷ ______.

Mike: Of course, but you still need to leave some of this behind.

Stacey: I know, but deciding what I don't need is a ❸ ______.

Mike: Well, think about what you will be doing on your trip.

Stacey: Um, I'll be going to a ❹ ______, and I'm going to be ❺ ______ in the jungle. That's why I've got my hiking ❻ ______.

Mike: OK, sure. Will you be relaxing at all?

Stacey: Definitely. I will be ❼ ______ on the beach for a few days after I arrive, so I need to take a ❽ ______ of swimsuits.

Mike: That makes sense, but I'm sure you don't need two sweaters and two pairs of jeans. Take one of each just in case the weather gets ❾ ______ one day. Also, you should leave behind some of those T-shirts. You won't need all five of them if you're going to be lying on the beach.

Stacey: Yeah, OK. I guess you're right. If I take out this ❿ ______ pair of sneakers as well, I should be able to fit everything in.

Words to Remember

Use the words in the box to complete the sentences.

eventuality	*struggle*	*cram*	*wildlife park*	*trek*
gear	*chill out*	*choice*	*chilly*	*spare*

1. I have a lot of work to do, and it will be a ______ to get everything finished.
2. I ______ a lot of food into my lunch box in case I get hungry.
3. Sally took the day off work, so she's ______ at home.
4. I lost my keys, but I have a ______ set at home.
5. If you want to go ______ through the forest, you need a good pair of boots.

Get It Right

A. Scan the following brochure for a vacation. Familiarize yourself with the writing style.

We're very happy you signed up for the Australian Coastal Adventure Vacation; it's one of the most exciting trips you can go on. You'll be spending a lot of time in the water, so make sure you pack more than one swimsuit. You should also expect to be in the sun a lot, so bring a hat and sun cream. A good pair of hiking boots is important as you'll be hiking through forests. This trip isn't just about adventure, though. You'll be staying in luxury hotels that have great bars and restaurants, so women might want to pack a couple of dresses and men should bring shirts and pants.

B. Imagine you are a travel agent and you have to write about a special vacation and tell travelers what they should pack to take with them.

Grammar Bite

We mainly use the Future Continuous tense to talk about actions that will be in progress in the future.

A. Statements

1. will be V-ing I ***will be*** playing soccer tomorrow	2. am / are / is going to be V-ing I ***am going to be*** painting next weekend.

B. Questions

1. will sb. be V-ing? • ***Will*** you ***be*** coming tomorrow? 2. Am / Are / Is sb. going to be V-ing? • ***Are*** you ***going to be*** singing again?	3. What will sb. be V-ing? • What ***will*** you ***be*** doing later? 4. What am / are / is sb. going to be V-ing? • What ***are*** they ***going to be*** eating for dinner?

Give It a Try

Use the Future Continuous tense to answer or complete the questions.

1. What are you going to be doing tomorrow?

____

2. What will you be doing next weekend?

____

3. Q: What ______________________________?

A: He will be studying this evening.

4. Q: What ______________________________?

A: They are going to be watching cartoons.

Prepare Yourself

Look at the pictures of vacation activities below. Talk with your partner about what you will be doing on your next vacation.

Activity 1

Based on what you are going to be doing, what will you need to pack for your vacation? How much money will you need to prepare? Discuss with your partner.

Activity 2

When you've decided what you will take with you, talk to your partner about what things you will put in your main luggage and what you will put in your hand luggage.

Main luggage	Hand luggage
______________	______________
______________	______________
______________	______________

Useful Expressions

- For money, I will *take traveler's checks* and *cash*.
- I will pack *a swimsuit* because I will be *going to the beach*.
- I'll probably want my *book* on the flight, so I will put it in my hand luggage.
- I will put my *camera* in my luggage since I won't need it until I arrive.

Unit 3

Meeting Other Travelers

By the end of this unit, you will be able to do the following:

- Introduce yourself and others
- Plan a "meet and greet"
- Make a good first impression
- Describe your personality

Before We Go

When you go on vacation, especially if you join a tour group, you'll meet a lot of new people with different characteristics. Look at the pictures of people below and use the list of characteristics from the box to describe what each person is like.

outgoing	*shy*	*thoughtful*	*funny*
serious	*childish*	*gloomy*	*arrogant*

1 __________

2 __________

3 __________

4 __________

5 __________

6 __________

7 __________

8 __________

Useful Expressions

- You'll *love* him; he's always so *funny*.
- She can be a little *childish*, but she is *nice*.
- He's usually *shy* when he *first meets people*, but that changes when he *gets to know them*.

Conversation 1

Track 8 Tom joined a tour group to travel around India. On the first night of his vacation, the members of the group meet in the hotel bar to get to know each other. Tom starts chatting with a lady called Olivia. Listen to the conversation and fill in the missing words.

Tom: Hi, there. I'm Tom.

Olivia: I'm Olivia. It's nice to meet you.

Tom: Yeah, you too. I can't believe I'm in India. I'm so excited about the tour.

Olivia: That makes two of us. Coming here is a ❶ ________ dream for me, and I think the next two weeks are going to be ❷ ________.

Tom: I couldn't agree more. What are you most looking forward to?

Olivia: That's ❸ ________ impossible to answer; there are so many things. Seeing the Taj Mahal will be a magical experience, but I think the best thing could be ❹ ________ another culture and ❺ ________ the local food.

Tom: Ah, I'm not so sure about that. I'm not really ❻ ________ to eating spicy food.

Olivia: I'm worried for your stomach then. I hope you won't be stuck in the bathroom for the ❼ ________ trip!

Tom: You and me both! Anyway, have you been away with a tour group before?

Olivia: No, this is my first time. I was a bit ❽ ________ about doing it as I'm usually shy and quiet around people I don't know.

Tom: I wouldn't say that; you seem very ❾ ________. Anyway, I think it's sometimes nice to meet new people. At least we know we won't feel ❿ ________ on our vacation.

Olivia: That's true, and after meeting you, I feel that I've made one friend already!

Words to Remember

Use the words in the box to complete the sentences.

lifelong	*sample*	*unforgettable*	*practically*	*witness*
accustom	*entire*	*reluctant*	*chatty*	*lonely*

1. Tom comes from Brazil, and he's not ________ to London's cold weather.
2. When the boy started at a new school, he didn't know anyone and felt very ________.
3. Joe must have been hungry. He ate the ________ pizza in about 15 minutes!
4. Amy got a score of 99 on the test. She got ________ every question correct.
5. Kelly felt very upset after ________ the accident.

Reading

Track 9 **Olivia was worried about meeting new people on her vacation, so before she went away, she looked for advice on how to make a good first impression. Read the information she found. How much of it did you already know?**

Making a good first impression

Many of us worry about meeting people for the first time, but if you follow a few simple rules, you can almost always make a good first impression.

1. Be aware of body language

Folding your arms will make you look cold and unfriendly, so put your hands in your pockets or place one on your hip. Also, stand up straight to make yourself seem sure of yourself.

2. Smile and maintain eye contact

Smiling at someone when you say hello gives the impression that you're happy to meet them. Looking at them while they're speaking to you helps to show that you're interested in what they have to say. Make sure you don't stare, though – look away from their eyes occasionally.

3. Don't tell too many jokes

They're probably not as funny as you think they are. Even if you do know some great jokes, using them on a first meeting will make other people think you'll tell jokes every time you chat.

4. Ask questions

Get the other person to talk about themselves, and ask questions that are appropriate for the situation. If you meet someone on vacation, ask if they're having a good time or why they decided to come to that place.

5. Finish the conversation well

Make the other person feel good about your conversation, so tell them that you enjoyed meeting them. It will make them feel that they could come and talk to you again.

Give It a Try

Read the advice again and circle *True* or *False* for each statement.

1. You will look confident if you stand up straight. True / False
2. You should look at someone most of the time when talking to them. True / False
3. When in a sports event, it's fine to ask about someone's future plan. True / False
4. You should say something nice to end the conversation. True / False
5. It's better to fold your arms when meeting someone for the first time. True / False

Conversation 2

Track 10 A few days later, Tom has met everyone in his tour group and is chatting with Ruth about the trip and the other travelers. Listen to the conversation and fill in the missing words.

Tom: I've only been in India for three days, but I already think this is hands down the best vacation I've ever had.

Ruth: I know, and dinner last night was to die for, wasn't it? The chef cooked the lamb beautifully.

Tom: It was ❶ ______. I also loved the ❷ ______ we saw yesterday.

Ruth: They were amazing weren't they? They looked ❸ ______ good in the evening; they seemed so mysterious in the ❹ ______.

Tom: Everything we've seen has been ❺ ______, but meeting everyone on the tour has been the icing on the cake for me.

Ruth: That reminds me, I saw you chatting to Olivia last night. I haven't really spoken to her yet; what's she like?

Tom: She can be a bit shy and ❻ ______ at first; that's why she often talks very quietly. But we ❼ ______ well now, and I find her very easy to talk to.

Ruth: I guess I must have gotten the wrong ❽ ______ of her. I ❾ ______ she was a very serious person.

Tom: In some ways she is, but she's also very funny, and she's ❿ ______ smart; she knows so much about the places we're visiting on this trip.

Ruth: That's interesting. It just goes to show that you can't judge a book by its cover.

Tom: That's definitely true. I think she's waving to me to go and chat with her. Why don't you come with me?

Ruth: I'd like that.

Words to Remember

Use the words in the box to complete the sentences.

sensational	*palace*	*especially*	*moonlight*	*memorable*
reserved	*get along*	*impression*	*assume*	*incredibly*

1. I don't talk to him very much. We don't really ______ well.
2. That movie was ______. I could happily watch it again tomorrow.
3. The rich king has ______ all over the country.
4. The student ______ she had passed the test, so she was disappointed when she was given a low grade.
5. He's quite ______ so it might take you a long time to get to know him well.

Get It Right

A. Scan the following letter for a meet-up event. Familiarize yourself with the writing style.

Hi, everyone

We're going to have a fun "meet and greet" in the hotel lobby this evening, and it would be great to see you all there. We'll start at 8 p.m. with a few games – don't worry, you won't be asked to do anything embarrassing – and then we'll all relax and casually enjoy some wine and snacks. It doesn't matter if you're loud and outgoing or quiet and reserved, you'll be able to have a nice evening. Also, getting to know people and making a few friends will help you enjoy your vacation more fully.

You can join or leave the event whenever you like, but it would be great to see you!

Pete (Tour Leader)

B. Imagine you are organizing a "meet and greet" activity for the members of a tour group. You want everyone to get to know each other well. What would you say about the event?

Grammar Bite

Generally, adjectives describe nouns and adverbs describe verbs. You can often make adverbs by adding *-ly* to an adjective, but there are some irregular adjectives and adverbs that don't follow this rule.

A. Regular adjectives and adverbs

1. **Add *-ly***
   - The boy *sadly* looked at the rain and knew he couldn't play outside.
2. **Change *y* to *i*, add *-ly***
   - She always sings so *happily*.

B. Irregular adjectives and adverbs

1. **Adverbs without *-ly***
   - They speak English very *well*. NOT They speak English very goodly.
2. **Adverbs with the same form as adjectives**
   - He drives too *fast*.
3. **Adjectives without adverb forms**
   - She is feeling *lonely* today.
   - I try to be *friendly* with everyone.

Give It a Try

Decide whether each word is an adjective or adverb. Then use it to write a sentence

Word	Adjective or adverb	Sentence
proudly		
lovely	Adjective	You have a lovely home!
excitedly		
tired		

Prepare Yourself

Imagine you're on a tour group vacation and have to introduce yourself to another traveler. What kind of person are you?

Characteristics

mischievous

quick-tempered

humorous

sensitive

Hobbies

handicrafts

reading

watching movies

playing sports

Activity 1

Introduce yourself to your partner. When your partner is speaking, ask questions to get as much information as possible.

Activity 2

Look at the descriptions of the three people pictured below. Talk to your partner about which one you'd like the most.

Jenny	Mike	Rachel
• I'm sweet and caring. • I like cooking. • I'm really looking forward to experiencing another culture.	• I'm laid-back and thoughtful. • I like music and sports. • The thing I'm looking forward to most is seeing India's amazing sights.	• I'm cool and fun-loving. • I enjoy going out and partying with friends. • I'm most looking forward to sampling the local nightlife.

Useful Expressions

- I'm a fairly *thoughtful* person.
- One of my biggest interests is *sport*. I love *tennis*.
- I think I'd like *Mike* the most. We seem to have a lot in common.
- I'd get along well with *Rachel*. She seems really interesting.

Units 1-3
REVIEW 1

Listening

A. Track 11 Listen to the speakers and choose the best responses.

1. **a.** Yes, I think this trip will be great.
   b. No, it's too risky. I will just use my credit card.
   c. No, I always pack the cash in my luggage.
   d. Yes, I brought a lot of traveler's check just in case.
2. **a.** Why not? That kind of trip allows you to see something new.
   b. I agree. I wouldn't want to travel on a ship all the time.
   c. You're right. That way, you get to see other people's lifestyles.
   d. Really? I actually thought the trip was pretty boring.
3. **a.** That kind of trip allows me to meet different people.
   b. That kind of trip offers the chance to relax and learn things.
   c. I like it because I can avoid the traffic on the roads.
   d. I like it because it offers me more opportunities to exercise.

B. Track 12 Listen to the short conversation. Then, circle *True* or *False* for each sentence.

1. This conversation is probably a phone call to a travel agency. True / False
2. The woman will recommend that the man go on an adventure trip. True / False
3. The man will pobably receive some travel itineraries in his e-mail. True / False

C. Track 13 Listen to the short talk and choose the best answer to each question.

1. Which of the following is true?
   a. Mom should go to the bank and get some traveler's checks.
   b. There will be fine dining on the trip, so fancy dresses are important.
   c. Using credit cards is safer than carrying huge amounts of cash.
   d. The travelers will be doing a lot of sightseeing around the hotel.
2. What can we tell about the caller?
   a. He is an inexperienced traveler.
   b. He is not sure his mom will remember everything.
   c. He will be taking care of his mom's passport.
   d. He wants to have a very fancy trip.

Vocabulary

Use the words in the box to complete the following sentences.

extend	*struggle*	*commission*	*serious*	*assume*	*rental*	*laid-back*

1. I ❶ ______ that the man was very unfriendly. I guess first impressions are not always correct.
2. If you want to ❷ ______ your vacation, be sure to change the departure date of you flight.
3. I damaged the ❸ ______ bicycle after I accidentally hit a rock.
4. I don't like using traveler's checks because you have to pay a ❹ ______.
5. My last vacation was very ❺ ______. I relaxed by the pool and had a few massages.
6. It will be a ❻ ______ to get everything done, so we should pack together.
7. Those women seem to be very ❼ ______. It's probably not a good idea to make jokes around them.

Reading

Complete the words in the text. The first letters are given.

Hi, Trevor,

My name is Lara Staden, we met briefly on the cruise last week. I'm writing because I wanted to apologise for being rude to you at the dinner party.

I'm usually a very fri______ and out______ person, and I enjoy meeting and chatting to new people. I generally get along with people very well. However, before the party, I ran into a very arr______ woman who criticized my dress. I felt very upset and felt that way for the entire evening. Before you came over to talk to me, I saw her talking to you. I ass______ that you were close friends and thought you must be similar people. That's why I walked away before you finished speaking. After the party, our mutual friend Sharon came to me and told me that after witnessing the whole thing, she thought I had jumped to conclusions. She said that you are actually a very polite and tho______ person, and that you really wanted to get to know me.

I felt very bad about this, so I thought I should write to say sorry. Also, as an apology, I would like to in______ you to lunch sometime next week. Please let me know when you will be available. I hope we'll have a chance to get to know each other better.

Sincerely,

Lara

Unit 4

Checking In / Out

By the end of this unit, you will be able to do the following:

- Check in to and check out of a hotel
- Talk about services offered in a hotel
- Requesting things from the hotel receptionist
- Discuss the details of a hotel bill

Before We Go

When you check in to and out of a hotel, you'll almost certainly find the check-in desk in the hotel lobby. Look at the list of things you'll see in a lobby and use the terms to label the pictures.

check-in desk	*concierge*	*luggage cart*	*bar*
escalator	*bellhop*	*information desk*	*elevator*

❶ ______

❷ ______

❸ ______

❹ ______

❺ ______

❻ ______

❼ ______

❽ ______

Useful Expressions

- I have a room reserved under the name *Amy Roberts*.
- I'd like to check in, please. I booked *a double room*; it's in the name of *Singh*.
- I'd like to check out of *Room 213*.

Conversation 1

Track 14 Emma has arrived at her hotel and is ready to start her vacation. First, she needs to check in to her hotel. Listen to the conversation and fill in the missing words.

Receptionist: Hello, madam. How may I help you?

Emma: Hi, I'm here to check in. My room's booked under the name Emma Mason.

Receptionist: OK, let me check that for you… Yes, I have you down for the starlight ❶ ______. Is that correct?

Emma: Yes, that's right.

Receptionist: Excellent. What that means is that you'll have free ❷ ______ to the hotel's ❸ ______ ❹ ______ throughout your stay. And I can see that you'll be with us for 14 nights and that you're booked into a ❺ ______ single room.

Emma: Yes.

Receptionist: OK, as part of your package, you are ❻ ______ to have breakfast in the Sunrise Room every day. Breakfast will be served from 6:30 to 10:30 every morning, and you'll find the Sunrise Room on the second floor.

Emma: Do I need any ❼ ______ to get breakfast?

Receptionist: No, just give your room number to whoever serves you. Here's your ❽ ______; you're in Room 314, which you'll find on the third floor. The elevators are over on your left.

Emma: Great, thank you! Oh, what time do I need to check out?

Receptionist: We ask guests to check out of the hotel by noon on the day of their ❾ ______.

Emma: Is there any chance I can check out at 2 p.m.? I'll be out all morning on that day, and I'd like to ❿ ______ before I check out.

Receptionist: Yes, I will arrange that for you. Enjoy your stay, Ms. Mason.

Emma: Thank you.

Words to Remember

Use the words in the box to complete the sentences.

spa	*freshen up*	*voucher*	*standard*	*key card*
access	*entitle*	*facility*	*package*	*departure*

1. Do you want to go to the café? I have a ______ for a free cup of coffee.
2. Could I use your bathroom? I need to ______ after my long journey.
3. I'm stuck in the airport. My plane's ______ time was delayed due to bad weather.
4. You can't go in that room. Only staff members have ______.
5. I can't wait to have a massage in the ______.

Reading

Track 15 **When Emma got to her room, she found a small basket of fruit and a welcome card waiting for her. Read the card and pay attention to the information it contains.**

Dear Guest,

On behalf of all the staff, I want to welcome you to the Golden Sands Hotel. I hope that your time here will be enjoyable in every way possible. Everyone who works at the hotel is expected to follow the highest standards; if you notice any member of staff who doesn't fulfill their duties properly, please tell me or someone on the front desk.

I want to remind you that we do have an excellent spa at the hotel, and specially trained staff are able to give you a range of massages and treatments. For an appointment, visit the spa or call them by dialing 8.

The hotel has two pools, and guests can also relax on the beach next to the hotel. Please don't take bathroom towels to the pool or beach. Instead, go to the pool cabin and collect beach towels there.

To find out more about the hotel's facilities, including the children's play group, and in-room services, look in the services folder in the top drawer of your desk. You'll also find room service menus.

Please feel free to contact me if you have any problems or requests. Enjoy your vacation!

Liz Thompson

Customer Services Manager

ext. 214

Give It a Try

Read the card again and choose the best responses to each of the following questions.

1. What does Liz Thompson do at the hotel?
   - **a.** She works on the front desk.
   - **b.** She takes care of guests' problems.
   - **c.** She manages the hotel.
   - **d.** She cleans rooms.
2. What's the best way to find out about the hotel gym?
   - **a.** Look in the services folder.
   - **b.** Call Liz Thompson.
   - **c.** Walk through the hotel.
   - **d.** Go to the front desk to ask.
3. What do you know about the spa?
   - **a.** It's on the eighth floor of the hotel.
   - **b.** You have to call to make an appointment.
   - **c.** The staff only offer massages.
   - **d.** The staff have received training.
4. What is said about the hotel?
   - **a.** Beach towels can be taken to guest rooms.
   - **b.** Room service is only available in the evening.
   - **c.** It has its own private beach.
   - **d.** It provides activities for children.
5. Why would you call Liz Thompson?
   - **a.** You want to order room service.
   - **b.** You want to ask about the spa.
   - **c.** You want to make a complaint.
   - **d.** You want to ask for more towels.

Conversation 2

Track 16 At the end of her vacation, Emma goes to the lobby to check out of the hotel. Listen to the conversation and fill in the missing words.

Emma: Hi, there. I'm here to check out of Room 314. Here's my key card.

Receptionist: I can do that for you, but you should have checked out before noon. There's actually an extra ❶ ________ for guests who check out late.

Emma: I think there's been a mistake. When I checked in I was told that I would be able to do it later. Your colleague said that he would ❷ ________ it ________ for me.

Receptionist: I don't have any note of that. Do you remember the name of the person who checked you in?

Emma: No, I have no idea.

Receptionist: OK, well, I'm sure it's just a computer ❸ ________. To help me ❹ ________ the bill, did you have anything from the ❺ ________?

Emma: No, well, I did have the bottled water every day, but the ❻ ________ told me it was ❼ ________.

Receptionist: Yes, that's right. Well, your room was already paid for, but here's a list of your room service and bar charges. You might want to check it to make sure everything's correct.

Emma: That all looks good to me. Is it OK if I pay with cash?

Receptionist: Of course. The total ❽ ________ is $125.

Emma: Here you are.

Receptionist: Thanks. How was your stay at the Golden Sands? Was everything to your ❾ ________?

Emma: Yes, I've had a ❿ ________ time.

Receptionist: That's good to hear. We hope to see you again.

Words to Remember

Use the words in the box to complete the sentences.

bill	*minibar*	*satisfaction*	*calculate*	*complimentary*
maid	*glitch*	*fantastic*	*sort out*	*charge*

1. I like going to that bar because they always give ________ peanuts.
2. There have been a few ________ in the program, so we're a little behind schedule.
3. I was hoping you could ________ my computer. I'm having a few problems with it.
4. Can you ask the ________ to come back and clean the room later?
5. Drinks and snacks from the ________ are always expensive.

Get It Right

In Conversation 2, Emma had a problem when she tried to check out late. The problem was sorted out very easily, but imagine that you have a bigger problem that causes you a lot of trouble.

Write to the hotel manager to complain about a problem that happened because of something a hotel employee told you. Make sure you use reported speech to explain what that person told you.

Grammar Bite

Look at the following statements and how they can be modified to produce reported speech.

Reported speech forms		
Present Simple		Past Simple
"I feel ill."	→	She said she felt ill.
Present Continuous		Past Continuous
"I am going for a walk."	→	He said he was going for a walk.
Past Simple		Past Perfect
"We watched a movie."	→	They told me they had watched a movie.
Past Continuous		Past Perfect Continuous
"Tom was chatting to his friend."	→	He told me Tom had been chatting to his friend.
Present Perfect		Past Perfect
"I've been busy."	→	She said she had been busy.

Give It a Try

Look at the following statements and then turn them into reported speech.

1. **Woman**: I can finish the work on time.

2. **Man**: We haven't been to the restaurant yet.

3. **The boys**: We are going to play soccer later.

4. **Man**: They were writing their homework.

Prepare Yourself

People often worry about checking in to and out of hotels if they have to use a second language. To make it easier for yourself, prepare a list of the things you need to talk about. If the hotel receptionist doesn't mention it, you can ask them questions to make sure you have all the information you need.

Have a look at the lists below. Would you add anything to them?

Checking in

1. How many nights?
2. What kind of room?
3. What kind of package?
4. Am I entitled to a free breakfast?
5. What time is breakfast served?
6. ______________________
7. ______________________

Checking out

1. Checking out
2. How much does the bill add up to?
3. Do I agree with all the charges?
4. Do I have any complaints?
5. What's the best way to get to the airport?
6. ______________________
7. ______________________

Activity 1

Checking in With your partner, take turns being a hotel guest and receptionist.

Activity 2

Checking out Now pretend you want to check out of a hotel.

Useful Expressions

- What time will *breakfast* be served?
- What time does the *pool close in the evening*?
- I need to get to the *airport*. Can you tell me the quickest way to get there?
- How much would a taxi to *the train station* cost?

Unit 5 Room Service

By the end of this unit, you will be able to do the following:

- ✈ Order room service
- ✈ Respond to requests
- ✈ Make suggestions
- ✈ Fill out comments cards

Before We Go

In many hotels, you can order room service and have food brought to your room, but this usually isn't the only in-room service available. Take a look at the list of services below and use the terms to label the picture.

massage	*housekeeping*	*unpacking service*	*laundry*
in-room movie	*room service*	*luxury bath*	*Internet connection*

❶ ______

❷ ______

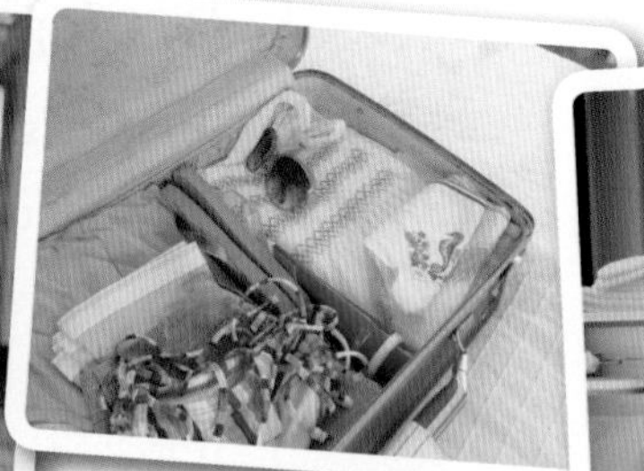

❸ ______

❹ ______

❺ ______

❻ ______

❼ ______

❽ ______

Useful Expressions

- I would love to have a *luxury bath*.
- I'm not interested in the *laundry service* because I *always pack enough clothes*.
- The *unpacking service* looks interesting. I might ask about that on my next vacation.
- I often use the *in-room movie* service in hotels.

Conversation 1

Track 17 **Scott checked in to his hotel a few hours ago and is now feeling hungry, so he decides to order some room service. Listen to the conversation and fill in the missing words.**

Scott: Hi, I'm in Room 713. I'd like to order some room service.

Hotel employee: Of course, sir. What can I get for you?

Scott: I'll have the chicken curry, please.

Hotel employee: I am sorry, but the chicken curry is on our daytime ❶ ______. After 9 p.m., we move to the night bites menu.

Scott: Oh, I see. Then I will order the steak and fries.

Hotel employee: Very well, and how would you like your steak to be cooked – ❷ ______, ❸ ______, or ❹ ______?

Scott: Medium, please, and can I get some ❺ ______ with that?

Hotel employee: Yes, we provide a ❻ ______ of sauces with all orders.

Scott: I think I'll get myself a ❼ ______ as well; I'm really hungry. Um, can I have a ❽ ______ of onion rings, please?

Hotel employee: Certainly. Would you like to order anything to drink or some dessert? I can ❾ ______ the chocolate cake.

Scott: Thanks, but I think I'll say no.

Hotel employee: OK, so that's a medium steak and fries with a side order of onion rings. We'll bring it to your room as soon as possible.

Scott: How long do you think it will be?

Hotel employee: Well, the kitchen is a little busy ❿ ______, so it might take about 25 minutes.

Scott: OK, that's fine. Thanks very much.

Words to Remember

Use the words in the box to complete the sentences.

side order	*selection*	*rare*	*portion*	*at the moment*
medium	*menu*	*well done*	*mustard*	*recommend*

1. This is an expensive restaurant. Nothing on the ______ costs less than $30.
2. If you're in London for a few days, I ______ going to see the Tower Bridge.
3. This hamburger has tomato sauce but no ______.
4. Can I call you back later? I'm finishing my homework ______.
5. These ______ are too small for me; I'm still hungry.

Reading

Track 18 **Later that evening, Scott wanted to relax and watch a movie, so he looked through the movies on offer on the hotel's in-room movie service list.**

IN-ROOM MOVIES

To watch a movie, go to the movie channel on your TV, use the arrows on the TV controller to select the movie you want, and press the red, "Enter" button. The first movie you see will cost you $7.50, and each movie after that will cost $5. You will be billed when you check out of the hotel.

LOVE IN THE NEWS Romantic comedy
STARRING MARK GRUFFALO AND REESE WITHERSPONGE

When Jeff Cooper (Gruffalo) moves to a new town and finds work with TV news company KPMG, he has to work with Anna Walker (Withersponge). At first, the two reporters hate each other and argue about everything. Then one day, they're involved in an accident and are forced to share a hospital room. While they're recovering, they realize how attracted to each other they are.

FREEFALL Action **STARRING TOM BRUISE**

Aging police officer Paul Mitchell (Bruise) is struggling to compete with his younger colleagues. He's not as strong or fast as them, and he worries that his age might stop him from catching the bad guys. However, when a crime boss tries to take over the city, the police need Mitchell's experience to stop him.

POLITICS ISN'T ENTERTAINMENT Drama
STARRING MATT DAMONE AND GEORGE BLOONEY

When Randy Bosch (Blooney), a millionaire businessman enters the running to become the next mayor of New York, some people say he's only doing it to make more money. Wayne Nilson (Damone), a popular radio DJ, decides to run against him and expose the crimes his businesses have committed.

THE ROACH Cartoon / Family **STARRING JOHN D. REILLY**

A cockroach named Hugo (Reilly) has problems making friends in a world where everyone judges people by how they look. At first, Hugo tries to pretend that he isn't a cockroach, but that leaves him unhappy. He later realizes that he needs to learn what his good characteristics are and accept himself for who he really is.

Give It a Try

Read the information again and choose the best responses to each of the following questions.

1. Which movie teaches people to feel good about themselves?
   a. *Freefall* **c.** *The Roach*
   b. *Love in the News* **d.** *Politics Isn't Entertainment*
2. How much would it cost to see all four movies?
   a. $5 **b.** $12.50 **c.** $20 **d.** $22.50
3. In *Love in the News*, when did the reporters fall in love?
   a. When they first met **c.** After they left hospital
   b. After they hurt themselves **d.** When they started working together
4. How would you see the movie you wanted to see?
   a. Choose it on your TV **c.** Make a phone call
   b. Get the DVD **d.** Visit the front desk
5. When would you pay for your movies?
   a. Before watching them **c.** When you leave the hotel
   b. After they finish **d.** The day after you watch them

Conversation 2

Track 19 **A week into his vacation, Scott feels stressed and decides to have a massage in his room. Listen to the conversation and fill in the missing words.**

Masseuse: I was told that you asked for the Rest and Relaxation Massage. Are you feeling ❶ ________?

Scott: I am, but I don't know why. I'm on vacation, which I've been saving for all year, and I should be having a good time.

Masseuse: It's actually quite ❷ ________ to feel tense on a vacation. People look forward to their trips for a long time and then worry that they're not having enough fun.

Scott: Oh, OK. That ❸ ________. I think I just need to relax and start enjoying myself.

Masseuse: You really should. Right, are there any joints or muscles that are giving you ❹ ________ trouble?

Scott: Yes, my neck and shoulders feel very tight. I've been ❺ ________ by them for a few days.

Masseuse: OK, and do you have any ❻ ________ that I should know about. I don't want to hurt you.

Scott: I do have problems with my left knee sometimes. I was hit by a car when I was crossing the road a few years ago.

Masseuse: That sounds terrible. I'll make sure that I'm very careful with your left leg.

Scott: I ❼ ________ that.

Masseuse: OK, why don't you go in the bathroom and put these clothes on? I'll stay out here and prepare the towels and oils for your massage.

Scott: That sounds great. I've never had a massage before; I'm looking forward to this.

Masseuse: Well, I think you'll find it very ❽ ________.

Words to Remember

Use the words in the box to complete the sentences.

soothing	*bother*	*make sense*	*tense*
appreciate	*common*	*particular*	*injury*

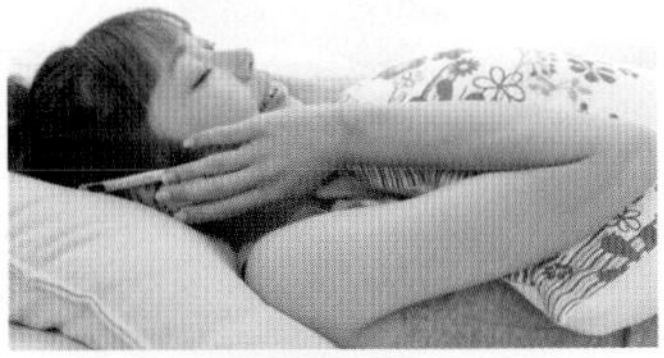

1. I often play this music before I sleep because it's so ________.
2. I ________ all the help you've given me this week.
3. It's ________ for young men to talk about which cars they'd like to drive.
4. I didn't agree with you before, but what you're saying ________.
5. I feel very bad about what happened last night. It has ________ me all night.

Get It Right

Many hotels leave "comments" cards in their guest rooms. People are asked to fill them in, giving their opinions on the hotel's services and employees. Imagine that you had received some good and bad in-room services and pretend to write about them on one of these cards. Try to use the passive voice in your comments.

I've had a great vacation, and I'd definitely come back and stay at your hotel. The most enjoyable thing about my time here was ...

____

____

____

Grammar Bite

Using the passive voice means that the focus of the sentence will be put on the object and not the subject. Passives can also be used when the subject is not known or is not important.

A. Creating the passive voice

1. am /are / is + past participle • The car *is cleaned* every day.	3. have / has been + past participle • The work *has been finished.*
2. was / were + past participle • The food *was cooked* yesterday.	4. had been + past participle • It *had been painted.*

B. Adding the cause of the action

You can add *by* to indicate the cause of the action. • The car is cleaned *by* the man every day. • The floor is mopped *by* the maid every morning.

Give It a Try

Look at the following pictures and write sentences about them using the passive voice.

1. every day

____

____

____

2. this morning

____

____

____

3. every week

____

____

____

4. last month

____

____

____

Prepare Yourself

There are so many different ways to relax or be entertained in your hotel room. Have a look at the pictures below and think about other services hotels offer.

gym

afternoon tea

conference

Activity 1

With your partner, discuss what kinds of in-room services are most useful and which ones you'd be most excited about getting.

Activity 2

Look at the room service menu below and decide what you want to order. Take turns placing orders with your partner.

Room Service Menu
Snacks
Fries $5
Cheese fries $6
Onion rings $6
Chicken nuggets .. $6
Vegetable bites $7
Main courses
Chicken curry $15
Vegetable curry $12
Fried rice $14
Fish and chips $18
Burger and chips ... $16
Cheese omelet $12
Desserts
Ice cream $6
Chocolate cake .. $8
Apple pie $10
Fruit tart $8

Useful Expressions

- I think it would be great to try the *luxury bath service* because *it would help me relax.*
- The most useful service would be the *Wi-Fi connection* because *many people take computers with them on vacation now.*
- I'd like to order *chicken nuggets* and *fried rice* please.
- Does the *apple pie* come with *ice cream*?

Unit 6 Hotel Facilities

By the end of this unit, you will be able to do the following:

- Use a business center
- Write a review
- Understand and create rules
- Overcome difficulties in hotels

Before We Go

In addition to in-room services, hotels provide a range of other services to keep their guests happy and comfortable. There are rooms and areas set aside for entertainment, business, sports and relaxation. Look at the list of services below, and use the terms to label the pictures.

gym	*business center*	*games area*	*restaurant*
sauna	*children's play area*	*lounge bar*	*hair and nails salon*

❶ ______

❷ ______

❸ ______

❹ ______

❺ ______

❻ ______

❼ ______

❽ ______

Useful Expressions

- Some hotels charge you for using the ***business center***, but others don't.
- I've never used a ***hotel spa***, so I don't know if they're free.
- *Gyms* are always free.
- *Hair and nails salons* can be quite expensive.

Conversation 1

Track 20 Rose went into the hotel business center to check her e-mails and write to her business partner.

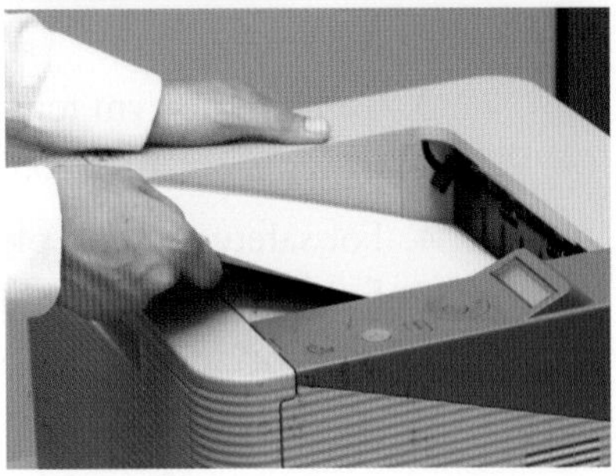

Hotel employee: Welcome to the business center. Would you like to use a computer?

Rose: Yes, please. Is it OK if I eat and drink in here?

Hotel employee: Of course. If you'd like, we even have ① ______ to make tea and coffee.

Rose: Great! I might have a cup later.

Hotel employee: Let me know if you need any ② ______.

Rose: Actually, I might. I need to print off some ③ ______. Is there a charge for doing that?

Hotel employee: There is. It's 25 cents ④ ______ page. When you ⑤ ______ the print ⑥ ______, you'll be asked for a ⑦ ______, which I'll give you later. As soon as you start printing, the charge ⑧ ______ gets added to your room bill.

Rose: OK, that sounds simple enough. Is there a time ⑨ ______ on how long I can use the computer for?

Hotel employee: There aren't any time limits. We just ask people to stay off ⑩ ______, entertainment sites, and games if it's busy in here.

Rose: I don't know why anyone would spend their vacations playing games in the business center.

Hotel employee: You'd be surprised. There are people who stay in here for hours.

Rose: Wow! Well, I'd better get started with my work, or I might be in here for hours myself. Thanks for your help.

Hotel employee: Not a problem.

Words to Remember

Use the words in the box to complete the sentences.

per	*limit*	*click on*	*automatically*	*document*
icon	*code*	*kettle*	*social network*	*assistance*

1. Rooms in this hotel cost $70 ______ night.
2. Thank you for your ______ today; I couldn't have done it without you.
3. The doors don't have handles. They ______ open when you walk towards them.
4. If you want to get money from an ATM, you need to enter a ______.
5. ______ the photo you want to see, and a larger version of it will appear on your screen.

Reading

Track 21 **During her stay at the hotel, Rose went to use the hotel gym. When she got inside, she saw a list of rules on the wall.**

Gym Rules

1. Do not eat in the gym.
2. Please feel free to use the blue towels while you're in the gym, but make sure you throw them in the towel basket when you leave.
3. To help the gym remain clean, please wipe equipment with a paper towel after you've finished using it.
4. For safety reasons, please put away weights after you've finished using them. Leaving weights lying on the floor can cause accidents.
5. If it's busy in the gym, please don't stay on one piece of equipment for too long. Also, please don't stand or sit on equipment that you aren't using.
6. If you're thirsty, paper cups are available next to the water machine, but please throw them away after using them.
7. If any of the machines are broken, or if you have any other problems, please contact a member of staff. If there are no hotel employees in the gym, use the phone and dial 7 to contact the front desk.
8. The gym will close every day at 10 p.m.

Enjoy your workout, and have fun getting fit!

Give It a Try

Read the notice again and choose the best responses to each of the following questions.

1. Why are people asked to put weights away?
a. To keep the gym tidy
b. To help the hotel staff
c. To help people use machines
d. To keep the gym safe

2. What are you asked to do to keep the gym clean?
a. Use the blue towels.
b. Wipe the equipment you've used.
c. Make sure your gym clothes are clean.
d. Don't take food into the gym.

3. What should you do if you don't know how to use a machine?
a. Ask a hotel employee.
b. Ask anyone in the gym.
c. Go to the hotel front desk.
d. Don't use the machine.

4. When are you asked not to use machines for too long?
a. In the evenings
b. Before the gym closes
c. When hotel employees aren't in the gym
d. When there are lots of people in the gym

5. What are you told to throw in the trash?
a. Water bottles
b. Blue towels
c. Water cups
d. Paper towels

Conversation 2

Track 22 Rose is bored one afternoon when the weather is bad, so she goes into the games room to see if there's anything fun she can do. She sees another hotel guest playing pool.

Rose: Oh, hi. I just came in to play pool. I don't suppose you'd like a game, would you?

Dean: I'm actually ❶ ________ at pool. I don't think you'd enjoy the game.

Rose: If it means I'll win easily, I might have fun. It could really ❷ ________ me ________.

Dean: Haha, well, we could play if you want, or we could have a game of ❸ ________ instead.

Rose: You're on! I used to love playing ping pong. Oh, there's a sign saying we need to hand in a room key at the front desk to get the ❹ ________ and ball. Wait for me. I'll be right back.

Dean: Sure, I'll be right here.

Rose: Right, I've got everything. The paddles look about ten years old, but they should be OK. Do you want a few shots to ❺ ________ first?

Dean: Not on my account; let's get on with the game. I'll let you ❻ ________.

Rose: You sound confident. I'm going to enjoy beating you.

Dean: Why don't we make this game more interesting? Whoever loses has to buy the winner a drink in the bar.

Rose: You bet! I haven't had a chance to ❼ ________ the bar yet anyway.

Dean: Well, this day is certainly ❽ ________ much better than I had expected.

Rose: I know what you mean. Now, are you ready to play?

Words to Remember

Choose the words in the box to complete the following sentences.

turn out	*paddle*	*cheer up*	*warm up*
check out	*serve*	*ping pong*	*dreadful*

1. The runners all ________ before taking part in the race.
2. Do you want to ________ the new Italian restaurant tonight?
3. You look so sad. I wish there was something I could do to ________ you ________.
4. I thought I had a big test today, but it ________ that the teacher wants to do it next week.
5. I don't like Eddie. He said some ________ things about my dress yesterday.

Get It Right

There are lots of hotel review sites on the Internet. Imagine you've just stayed in a hotel and want to write a review about the facilities.

I just stayed at the Merlin Hotel, and I had a wonderful time. The room was very nice, and the facilities were excellent. I tried out the spa on my first day,...

Grammar Bite

Phrasal verbs are made by combing verbs with prepositions or adverbs. Their meanings are often completely different to the meanings of the verbs on their own. Some phrasal verbs are intransitive, meaning that they don't have direct objects. For example:

come back → return

- *Come back* quickly.

make out → progress

- Let me know how you *make out*.

Some phrasal verbs with direct objects are separable, meaning that the object can come between the verb and the preposition or adverb.

Separable phrasal verbs	Inseparable phrasal verbs
pick up • *Pick up* the ball. / *Pick* the ball *up*. let down → disappoint • I didn't want to *let* the girl *down*. / I didn't want to *let down* the girl	go over → review • He will *go over* his exam. settle on → choose • He didn't know what to order but *settled on* the pasta.

Give It a Try

Make sentences with the following phrasal verbs. Their meanings are given in parenthesis.

Intransitive phrasal verbs	Separable phrasal verbs	Inseparable phrasal verbs
show up (arrive) What time do you think he will show up?	wear out (use until broken)	drop out of (quit)
turn in (go to bed)	stand up (don't go to a meeting)	keep at (keep going with)

Prepare Yourself

Hotel facilities such as gyms, business centers, and games areas often have rules. Take a look at these examples and think about what kind of facility they apply to.

Activity 1

With your partner, choose a hotel service and then decide whether it should have any rules. If you think you don't need to make any rules, explain why.

Activity 2

Look at the situations below. Talk to your partner about what each person should do to overcome their problem. What would you most likely do if you were in the same situation?.

Paul
The running machine isn't working.

Eddie
The hot tub isn't hot.

Mike
There aren't any pool cues next to the pool table.

Useful Expressions

- We should tell people not to *eat* in the *gym* because *it will get the room dirty*.
- There should be *a limit* on how long people can use the computers in the business center.
- I don't think *lounge bars* need rules; everybody knows what they're supposed to do there.
- *Paul* should *ask whether the machine can be fixed. He might have to go to the front desk.*
- If I were him, I would probably *just ignore the problem and use a different machine.*

Units 4-6
REVIEW 2

Listening

A. Track 23 Listen to the speakers and choose the best responses.

1. a. No, I wouldn't want people to see the contents of my luggage.
   b. Yes, I never know how to pack my stuff properly.
   c. Yes, I think it's a good idea to take it off the service list.
   d. No, this service should really be free of charge.
2. a. No, I don't know if they are free.
   b. Yes, I usually have to leave a tip afterwards.
   c. No, I think most of them are free of charge.
   d. Yes, they are suitable for guests of all ages.
3. a. I have a room reserved under the name Nancy Timmons.
   b. No, I'd like to check out of room 2213.
   c. Yes, I need to stay for two extra nights.
   d. It was fantastic. I especially enjoyed breakfast buffet.

B. Track 24 Listen to the conversation and choose the best answers to each question.

1. Who might the speakers be?
   a. A guest and a hotel worker
   b. Guests staying at the same hotel
   c. People who want to work at a hotel
   d. Guests waiting to use the business center
2. Which of the following is not true?
   a. The woman has tried all the services.
   b. The man might need to use the business center.
   c. There are some free services in the hotel.
   d. The business center might not be free.
3. What will happen next?
   a. The woman will go to the gym.
   b. The receptionist will talk about special offers.
   c. The man will talk to a hotel worker.
   d. The hotel will provide more free services.

Vocabulary

Circle the correct word to complete the sentences.

1. I want to go for a massage; I feel very ***(tense / bothered)*** after the long bus trip.
2. Do you know what time the ***(spa / minibar)*** closes on weekends?
3. You have to ***(turn out / check out)*** the hotel's lounge bar sometime; it's beautiful.
4. There is a huge ***(selection / portion)*** of dishes to choose from in this restaurant.
5. Be sure to return the key card upon your ***(satisfaction / departure).***
6. Just dial "0" for the reception if you need any ***(assistance / documents).***

Reading

Fill in the blanks with the correct answers below.

Hello, Mr. Jones. My name is Helen, I'm the ① ________ from Sunrise Hotel and Resort. I would like to thank you for choosing to stay with us again. We will send a drink and some fruit up to your room to help you ② ________ from your long flight. Finally, since you are a VIP guest, you have unlimited ③ ________ to all of the facilities, so feel free to use them. We hope you will find our services satisfactory.

1. **a.** concierge **b.** receptionist **c.** maid **d.** porter
2. **a.** sort out **b.** check in **c.** freshen up **d.** turn in
3. **a.** charges **b.** vouchers **c.** packages **d.** access

Writing

Rewrite the sentences according to the instructions in the parenthesis.

1. Jenny is dancing. Sally told me. (Reported speech)

   ____

2. If you click the icon on, you can print the document out. (fix the sentence)

   ____

3. Henry cleans the bedroom every weekend. (Passive; Present Simple)

   ____

Unit 7

All About Breakfast

By the end of this unit, you will be able to do the following:

- Discuss breakfast options
- Order eggs
- Advertise a restaurant
- Make quick requests

Before We Go

Many hotels provide large, all-you-can-eat breakfasts with a range of hot and cold dishes from many different countries placed around the dining room. Have a look at the list of foods below and use the names to label the foods.

cereal	*pancake*	*sausage*	*baked beans*
bacon	*croissant*	*scrambled eggs*	*hash brown*

❶

❷

❸

❹

❺

❻

❼

❽

Useful Expressions

- I like to eat *sausages*, *fried eggs*, and *hash browns*, but I know they're *unhealthy*.
- I usually start my day with *cereal* because *it tastes good and gives me energy*.
- I love *croissants*, and I don't often get to have *them* at home.

Conversation 1

Track 25 Owen goes to the hotel dining room one morning to get breakfast. Listen to the conversation and fill in the missing words.

Hotel employee: Good morning, sir. What room are you staying in?

Owen: Room 217.

Hotel employee: OK. Are you eating alone this morning or will somebody be joining you?

Owen: My wife will be here in a few minutes.

Hotel employee: OK, then if you'd like to follow me, I'll show you to a table for two. Can I ❶ ________ you any tea or coffee?

Owen: Two coffees, please – black.

Hotel employee: Not a problem. I'll bring them to you soon. If you need a ❷ ________ later on, just ask any of the ❸ ________ or ❹ ________. Whenever you're ready, help yourself to whatever food you might want. You'll find plates, bowls, and ❺ ________ around the room.

Owen: That's great. Oh, what time do you stop serving food?

Hotel employee: The chefs stop cooking food at 10:00, and we begin ❻ ________ the food containers at 10:30.

Owen: Ah, that doesn't give us much time. We had a bit of a ❼ ________ today.

Hotel employee: Well, you're on vacation; you should ❽ ________ yourself and ❾ ________.

Owen: That's right. Just one more thing before you go, could we get another ❿ ________? There's only one on the table.

Hotel employee: Sorry about that. I'll bring one with your coffee.

Words to Remember

Use the words in the box to complete the sentences.

treat	*waiter*	*cutlery*	*napkin*	*take it easy*
refill	*waitress*	*fetch*	*lie-in*	*clear away*

1. Could you ________ me the cookies from the kitchen, please?
2. The father ________ his children to a trip to Disneyland.
3. ________! Don't get so angry.
4. Would you bring me a new knife and fork, please? My ________ is dirty.
5. I'd like to have a ________ to catch up on sleep on the weekend.

Reading

Track 26 People say breakfast is the most important meal of the day, and it's important to make sure you get something healthy. Read the advice below on how to get a healthy breakfast, and look up any words you don't understand.

Start Your Day Right

No matter what you're going to be doing for the rest of the day, it's important that you get a good breakfast. You need something that will give you energy and get your stomach working.

Foods that are high in fiber are great as they not only help you go to the toilet, but also reduce the risk of you developing health problems like heart disease or cancer. If you're unsure what foods contain fiber, look for things with whole grains like brown bread, brown rice, and porridge. Fruits and vegetables are also good sources of fiber.

Another reason fruit is good at breakfast time is that it has lots of natural sugar, so it will give you a quick energy boost. Another important kind of food is protein, as this is used by your body to create new muscle. Protein can be found in lots of foods including meat, fish, eggs, cheese, and beans.

If you like cereal, be careful which one you buy, as many of them contain lots of sugar, which is bad for your teeth and could make you fat. You also have to be careful about how much fat you eat, so don't have too many fried breakfasts. They're bad for your weight and could leave you feeling tired and too full.

Finally, make sure you eat breakfast every day, even if you're trying to lose weight. Studies show that people who miss breakfast are actually more likely to put on weight.

Give It a Try

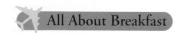

Read the advice again and choose the best responses to each of the following questions.

1. Why is it said that fruit is good?
   a. It gives you energy.
   b. It helps you lose weight.
   c. It's the best kind of breakfast food.
   d. It's quick to prepare.
2. What is NOT a source of protein?
   a. Chicken
   b. Apples
   c. Tuna fish
   d. Cheese
3. Why would fried eggs, fried tomatoes, and bacon be a bad breakfast?
   a. There's too much fat.
   b. There's no protein.
   c. There's too much fiber.
   d. There are no natural sugars.
4. What is said about cereal?
   a. They're all bad for you.
   b. They contain lots of fat.
   c. Be careful which ones you eat.
   d. They taste great.
5. According to the passage, why is fiber good for you?
   a. It helps you lose weight.
   b. It gives you energy.
   c. It's used to create muscle.
   d. It's good for your heart.

Conversation 2

Track 27 After Owen's wife arrives, he goes to get eggs for them both. Listen to the conversation and fill in the missing words.

Chef: Good morning, sir. How would you like your eggs today?

Owen: I'm not really sure. What are the different ways that I can have them?

Chef: Well, I make ❶ ________, fried eggs, and ❷ ________.

Owen: An omelet sounds good. Do they have any ❸ ________?

Chef: Yes, we have a selection of chopped tomatoes, onion, mushroom, and cheese, and you can choose whichever ones you want.

Owen: ❹ ________, can I have an omelet with tomatoes, onion, and cheese, please? And if I ask nicely, can you put three eggs in it?

Chef: This pan is only big enough for two eggs. If I put in three, they might spill out over the side. Sorry.

Owen: That's OK, but would you cook it very lightly? I don't like my eggs to be ❺ ________.

Chef: Don't worry, if I ❻ ________ it, I'll make you another one.

Owen: Thank you. I didn't ❼ ________ you made omelets. If I had known that before, I would have come here yesterday as well.

Chef: Well, I hope you enjoy it. I can see that you have two plates. Do you want eggs for someone else, as well?

Owen: Yes, could I get two fried eggs for my wife, please?

Chef: Certainly. Do you want them ❽ ________, ❾ ________, or ❿ ________?

Owen: Over easy, please.

Chef: Coming right up.

Words to Remember

Use the words in the box to complete the dialogue.

omelet	*filling*	*crispy*	*over easy*	*sunny side up*
realize	*lovely*	*overcook*	*over hard*	*scrambled eggs*

A: Do you ❶ ________ that we have now been dating for a year?

B: Yes, of course. I even bought a cake to celebrate. It has a chocolate ❷ ________.

A: ❸ ________! Do you remember the food I cooked for you on our first date?

B: I'll never forget! You left the meat in the pan too long and ❹ ________ it. It was so ❺ ________!

Get It Right

A. Scan the following advertisement for a restaurant.

If you're looking for somewhere new to eat breakfast, you should come to Oscar's. Our experienced chefs cook a variety of breakfast dishes from around the world including pancakes, waffles, English fried breakfasts, and Chinese congee. Our croissants, cereal, and toast are always fresh, and there's always plenty of tasty fruit if you want something healthy. If you need a lot of coffee to wake up in the morning, don't worry because at Oscar's, you can drink as much coffee as you want. We also offer free refills for tea and orange juice. If you come tomorrow, you might win something special, as we're giving away lots of great gifts.

We open at 6:30 a.m. every day, and we serve breakfast until 11 a.m.

B. Imagine you work for a restaurant that opens for breakfast. Write an advertisement for your restaurant and say how good the food is. You could also think of special offers that might get more people to eat there.

Grammar Bite

The first conditional is generally used to say what will happen if something else happens. If it's a mixed conditional, "will" can be replaced by "be going to" or certain modals. For example:

will • If you call, I ***will*** be happy. will → can • If you help me, I ***can*** finish the work. will → should • If you study, you ***should*** pass the test.	will → may • If you finish your cake, I ***may*** give you another piece. will → be going to • If you don't stop singing, I***'m going*** to leave.

In addition, the present simple verb in the "if" clause can be replaced by Present Continuous or Present Perfect verb.

- If you***'re meeting*** her, can you ask her to call me?
- If he***'s arrived***, you can tell him to come in.

Give It a Try

Connect the first part of each sentence with the correct endings.

_____ **1.** If you don't sleep, **a.** I will meet you.
_____ **2.** If you play every day, **b.** you should get better.
_____ **3.** If you pass the driving test, **c.** you can watch TV.
_____ **4.** If you've cleaned your room, **d.** you're going to be tired tomorrow.
_____ **5.** If you're coming tomorrow, **e.** you might lose weight.
_____ **6.** If you exercise, **f.** you can drive home.

Prepare Yourself

Large hotels often provide a wide range of dishes in their breakfast buffets. Try to identify the breakfast foods shown below and try to think of others.

Activity 1

What foods would you offer if you were a hotel manager? Choose ten foods, and then explain your decisions to your partner.

Activity 2

Read what the people introduced below like having for breakfast when they're on holiday and then talk to your partner about what you enjoy eating.

Phil When I'm on vacation I like to treat myself, so I usually get fried breakfasts with sausages, bacon, and eggs every morning. It may not be healthy, but it is delicious!

Sandy I like to try new things, so when I go to another country, I usually look for traditional, local breakfast foods.

Rose I'm never very hungry in the morning, but I know I should eat something, so I often just grab some fresh fruit. There's usually a good selection in hotels.

Useful Expressions

- I would offer *croissants* because I think they're delicious.
- I've chosen *cereal* because *millions of people eat it every morning*.
- I wouldn't have *waffles* because *I don't think they're breakfast foods*.

Unit 8

Making a Reservation

By the end of this unit, you will be able to do the following:

- Choose a restaurant
- Reserve a table
- Make an invitation
- Qualify your statements

Before We Go

Before making a reservation, you have to decide on what kind of restaurant you want to go to. Have a look at the list of restaurant types below and use the terms to label the pictures.

sushi bar	*French bistro*	*Indian restaurant*	*American diner*
pizzeria	*hot pot restaurant*	*vegetarian restaurant*	*seafood restaurant*

❶

❷

❸

❹

❺

❻

❼

❽

Useful Expressions

- I love *sushi bars*; the food is so *fresh and tasty*.
- I like going to *American diners* because *the atmosphere is usually very relaxed*.
- I'm not keen on *teppanyaki restaurants* because *I always come out smelling of food*.
- I'm a big fan of *curry*, so I go to *Indian restaurants* as often as I can.

Conversation 1

Track 28 Karen and Steve are looking through their guidebook, trying to find a great restaurant to eat dinner at. Listen to the conversation and fill in the missing words.

Karen: It says here that there's a good Thai restaurant near our hotel. Do you want to ❶ ________?

Steve: I'd rather not. My stomach hasn't felt good all day, and I'm worried that spicy food might make it worse.

Karen: Then I guess Indian food is out, too. What kind of food would you like?

Steve: Since we're near the sea, it would be great to ❷ ________ a really good seafood restaurant.

Karen: I know; the local fishermen are ❸ ________ very proud of their ❹ ________. I think we should have them at least once while we're here, but I don't ❺ ________ seafood tonight.

Steve: Are there any Italian places ❻ ________ in your guidebook?

Karen: I've seen one that looks ❼ ________ good, but it's a long way from the hotel and it would be quite difficult for us to get there.

Steve: It really shouldn't be this hard for us to find a good restaurant. Can I have a look at the book?

Karen: Yeah, here you are.

Steve: OK, ❽ ________ this place — Ronnie's American Diner? It says here that it has great burgers, pizza, apple pie, and ❾ ________. That sounds perfect to me.

Karen: Yeah, OK. I just hope they've got something ❿ ________ healthy on the menu. Give me the phone number and I'll call them to make a reservation.

Words to Remember

Use the words in the box to complete the sentences.

fancy	*fairly*	*milkshake*	*apparently*	*how about*
list	*lobster*	*try out*	*reasonably*	*give it a try*

1. If you want somewhere to go tomorrow, ________ the beach? The weather should be very good.
2. I'm so tired after work; I don't ________ going out tonight.
3. Susie asked me if I wanted to go to her exercise class, and I think I'm going to ________.
4. That restaurant is always busy because it offers fresh ________ caught from the sea.
5. I've never been there, but the food is ________ very good.

Reading

Track 29 **Many people use restaurant guides when they're in a new city or trying to find a new place to eat. Read the following passage, which is taken from a restaurant guide.**

London Dining

Papa Marco's

This traditional Italian restaurant has been serving food to appreciative customers for over 15 years. It's a family-run business, and everyone who works here is passionate about food and dining. Marco and his daughter, Stephanie, work in the kitchen while Marco's wife, Elaine, greets customers as they arrive. The menu constantly changes as Marco only uses fresh ingredients, but his tiramisu pudding is sold throughout the year and always tastes wonderful.

Pauline's Bistro

Pauline's Bistro has only been open for about six months, but it's already earned a reputation for excellent food. Most of the items on the menu are modern versions of traditional, local dishes, and they're all excellent. The only problem with the restaurant is the cost, as main dishes are priced at about \$40 to \$50 each. If you have plenty of money, though, you should give Pauline's a try.

The Roundhouse

The Roundhouse advertises itself as a restaurant offering cheap, simple food for the whole family, and that's exactly what it does. This isn't a place for fine dining, but if you just want a quick, tasty dinner, you won't be disappointed. It's also a good place to come if you're a vegetarian, as there are lots of suitable dishes on the menu. The waiters and waitresses are all very friendly, making this the perfect place for families.

Give It a Try

Read the guide again and choose the best responses to each of the following questions.

1. Where should you go if you don't eat meat?
- **a.** Papa Marco's
- **b.** The Roundhouse
- **c.** Pauline's Bistro
- **d.** Any of the above.

2. What do you know from the guide?
- **a.** Pauline's Bistro has been open a long time.
- **b.** The best food is at Papa Marco's.
- **c.** Stephanie is a waitress at Papa Marco's.
- **d.** The Roundhouse is cheaper than Pauline's Bistro.

3. What dish is recommended in the guide?
- **a.** A desert
- **b.** A soup
- **c.** A main course
- **d.** A burger

4. What kind of food is served at Pauline's Bistro?
- **a.** French food
- **b.** Italian food
- **c.** English food
- **d.** American food

5. What is said about The Roundhouse?
- **a.** The staff are very friendly.
- **b.** Its advertisement is not honest.
- **c.** Nobody leaves there disappointed.
- **d.** The food is not very good.

Conversation 2

Track 30 Karen picks up the phone and calls the restaurant to make a reservation. Listen to the conversation and fill in the missing words.

Waiter: This is Ronnie's American Diner, how can I help you?

Karen: I'd like to ❶ ______ a table for this evening, please.

Waiter: No problem, how many people will there be in your ❷ ______?

Karen: There are just two of us.

Waiter: OK. What time would you like your table for?

Karen: We'd like it quite early if that's OK. We're ❸ ______ to ❹ ______ soon, so we will have arrived by 5:30.

Waiter: That's OK; we can certainly serve you at 5:30, but I should warn you that the chefs won't have made the evening ❺ ______ by that time.

Karen: Oh, I think it would be a ❻ ______ to miss those. Maybe we can have a ❼ ______ around town and have dinner a bit later. What if we come in at 6:00; will that be OK?

Waiter: Yes, we will have started on the evening menu by then, so you'll be able to order whatever you want, including the specials.

Karen: Excellent. My name is Karen Taylor.

Waiter: OK, Ms. Taylor, I've reserved a table for two in your name for this evening at 6:00. We will ❽ ______ the table for you for 15 minutes, but if you're not here by 6:15 then we might give your table to other customers.

Karen: That's fine. I doubt we'll be late. I see in my restaurant guide that you have an ocean ❾ ______; could we have a table ❿ ______ the ocean?

Waiter: Yes, I'll make a note of that for you.

Karen: Excellent. See you later.

Waiter: See you later.

Words to Remember

Choose the words in the box to complete the following sentences.

party	*wander*	*book*	*view*	*head out*
intend	*shame*	*special*	*hold*	*overlook*

1. Joseph ______ to wake up at 6 a.m. tomorrow for a morning jog.
2. Tony would like a room that ______ the grand mountains.
3. I don't have any cash. Would you ______ this for me while I go find an ATM?
4. Carrie has ______ a room at the Regent Hotel for her honeymoon.
5. Can you wait me another 10 minutes? I'm not ready to ______ yet.

Get It Right

A. Scan the following invitation message. Familiarize yourself with the writing style.

Hi Rich,

I'm writing to invite you to a party we're having in the office next month. On October 4, Jodie Lipton will have worked here for 20 years, so we want to do something nice to celebrate the occasion. I know you and Jodie were always good friends, so it would be great if you could come in for the party. We're going to have the event on October 15. By then, the boss will have returned from his vacation, and everyone should have finished their current projects, so we'll all be able to relax. We'll be starting as soon as work finishes at 5:30. We hope to see you – I know you'd put a smile on Jodie's face!

Alex

B. Write a message to someone inviting them to a party or dinner. Include the reason why you're organizing the event, what time it will start and finish, and where it will be held.

Grammar Bite

The Future Perfect is used to talk about events or actions that will have been completed by a particular time in the future.

1. Positive statements	**will have + past participles** • I *will have read* the book by tomorrow. • He *will have taken* the test before Friday.
2. Negative statements	**will not / won't have + past participles** • They *won't have finished* yet.
3. Questions	**will + Subject + have + past participles** • *Will he have bought* the gift before the party?

Give It a Try

Change the following Future Simple sentences and questions into Future Perfect.

1. We will go to the park to play tennis.

____

2. Will you take the trash out tonight?

____

3. Amy will order the food in five minutes.

____

4. Sam is going to say sorry to her tomorrow.

____

5. I won't watch that movie.

____

Prepare Yourself

City guides are available in many tourist information offices. They often list a large number of restaurants and give each of them a one- or two-line review. Look at the city guide restaurant list shown below. Look up any words you don't know.

- **Bernie's Café** – cheap, greasy food.
  0327894638
- **Brushstrokes – elegant sushi bar, good food, reasonable prices.**
  0311895732
- **Canton Delight – affordable Chinese restaurant, friendly staff.**
  0348892513
- **Curry Heaven – slow service but delicious, spicy food.**
  0337800156
- **Dante – high-class Italian food.**
  0320914879
  Marty's – a classic American diner, family friendly.
  0377611098
  Pho – tasty, traditional Vietnamese dishes.
  0345531179
- **See Our Food – unattractive restaurant, but good food.**
  0324591190
- **Veggie Love – an exciting vegetarian menu**
  0333123466
- **Teppanyaki Town – popular teppanyaki restaurant, book ahead.**
  0345110929
- **XX Bistro – nice food, very entertaining restaurant manager.**
  0380792361

Activity 1

With your partner, decide which restaurant you would go to for a meal. Make sure it's somewhere you'll both be happy.

Activity 2

It's time to book your table. Take turns "calling" your partner to make a reservation. Remember to include the following things in your conversation:

- what time you want your table for
- how many people you want your table for
- special requests, eg., "I'd like a birthday cake brought to our table after our main course." "I'd like a table near the door."

Useful Expressions

- I like the look of *Pho*. I really enjoy *Vietnamese food*.
- I have a problem with *spicy food*, so I wouldn't want to go to *Curry Heaven*.
- How do you feel about *Veggie Love*? The *"exciting vegetarian menu" looks interesting*.
- I don't have much money, so I'd prefer somewhere less expensive like *Canton Delight*.
- A: Hello, this is *Brushstrokes*. How can I help you?
  B: I'd like to book / reserve a table for *three*.

Unit 9 Dining Etiquette

By the end of this unit, you will be able to do the following:

- Understand complicated dinner etiquette
- Identify the uses of different utensils
- Discuss cultural differences
- Suggest changes for better behavior

Before We Go

Does the sight of a fully set table in a high-class restaurant make you nervous? You're not alone. Try to match each word from the box with the appropriate item on the table to better understand the use of each plate, glass, and utensil.

wine glass	*dinner fork*	*salad fork*	*water glass*	*salad plate*
soup spoon	*dinner plate*	*dinner knife*	*napkin*	*table mat*

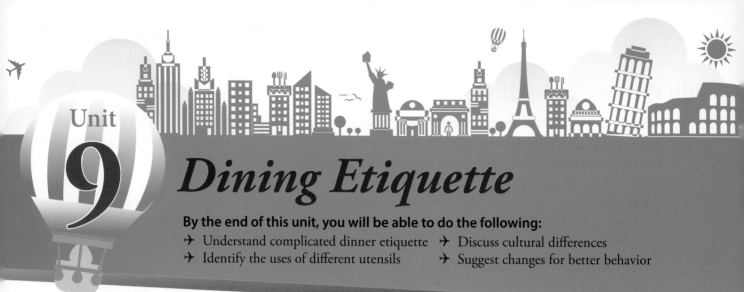

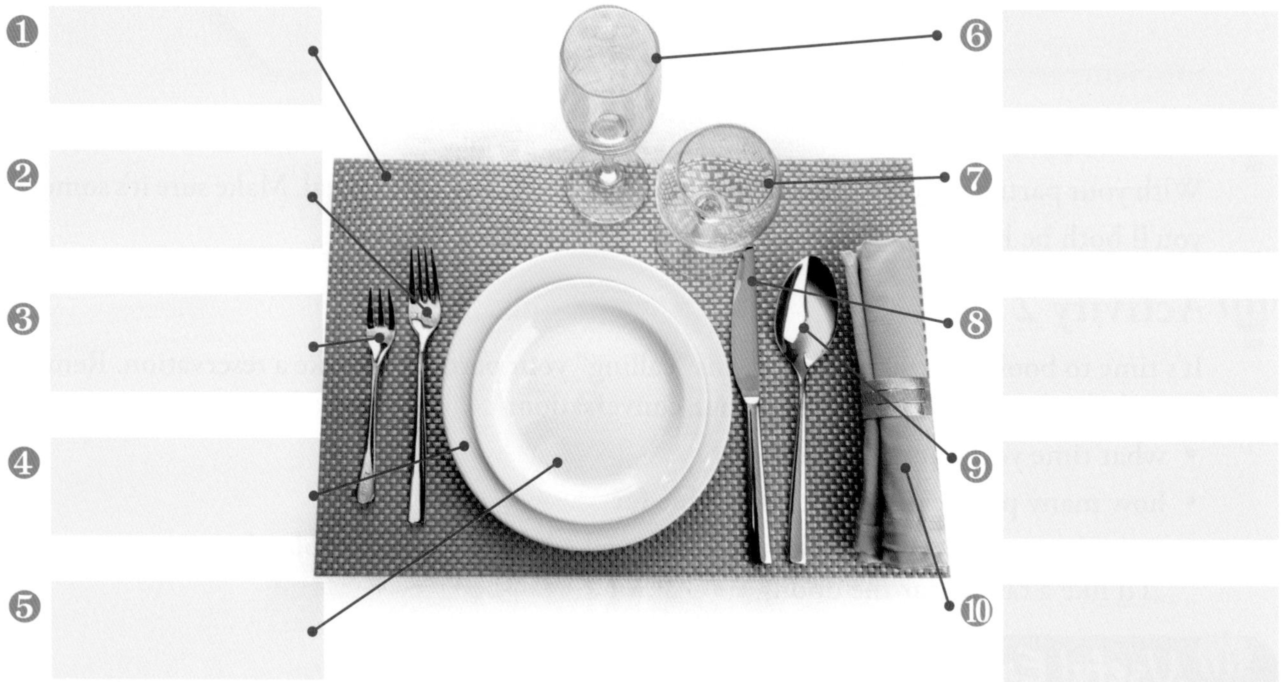

Useful Expressions

- In some countries, it's customary to *tip* waiters *10%*.
- I like fast-food restaurants because *they're fast and informal*.
- I think it's rude to *wear a hat in a restaurant*.

Conversation 1

Track 31 Robert is having dinner with Gail at a very nice restaurant in Rome. As they sit down, Robert is surprised by the amount of dining utensils, plates, and glasses on the table. Listen to the conversation and fill in the missing words.

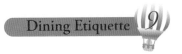

Robert: Wow! I did tell the waiter that it's just a table for two, right?

Gail: Yes. Don't feel ❶ ______ by the ❷ ______. It's easier to figure out than you think.

Robert: Could you give me a quick lesson before the waiter who took our order comes back? I don't want to ❸ ______ myself.

Gail: Well, ❹ ______, the glass that you just picked up is my water ❺ ______.

Robert: Oh! Sorry! What are these other glasses for?

Gail: The one that is closest to your right hand is for white wine. The bigger glass is for red wine. They're served with different ❻ ______.

Robert: What about all of this ❼ ______?

Gail: Just start with the fork that is on the outside and work your way in.

Robert: It's that simple? Is there anything else that I should know?

Gail: Well, it's considered ❽ ______ to put the ❾ ______ that is on your plate right now on your lap. If you get up from the table, put it on your chair until you return. Only put it on the ❿ ______ when you are finished with your meal.

Robert: That's good to know.

Words to Remember

Use the words in the box to complete the passage.

intimidate	*goblet*	*napkin*	*for starters*	*place setting*
course	*flatware*	*polite*	*embarrass*	*tablecloth*

Throwing a dinner party isn't easy, and many people are ______ by the experience. But you don't need to worry about ______ yourself; you just have to plan out everything carefully. ______, think about where you want people to sit — don't put lots of quiet people together because they might not talk. Put name cards on your ______ to make sure your guests know where they should sit. Then, think about the ______ you want to serve, and don't make anything you aren't confident about cooking.

Reading

Track 32 **Gail has let Robert borrow a book on dining etiquette. Read the excerpt below, and compare the information here to what you already know.**

When you're dining in the United States or Europe, whether you're at someone's home or in a fine restaurant, dining etiquette is very important. From the way you eat to which fork you use, the rules that govern dining etiquette should be learned.

Eating: Always chew with your mouth closed. Swallow the food that is in your mouth before you speak. Don't bring the bowl or plate that is holding your food to you; just use your fork or spoon to move one bite at a time to your mouth. Finally, wait until everyone has his or her food before you start eating the dish that you ordered.

Glasses: The wine or water glasses that belong to you will be to the right of your plate. Make sure you don't grab someone else's glass!

Passing: Do not reach across the table to get the salt or other item that you need. Ask the person who is nearest the item to pass it to you.

Cell phones: When you are dining at a restaurant, turn your phone's ringer off. If you need to take a call, leave the table and find a place where you won't disturb other diners with your talking.

Give It a Try

Read the excerpt again and choose the best response to each of the following questions.

1. What should you do when chewing food?
   - **a.** Thank your host.
   - **b.** Put your fork down.
   - **c.** Keep your mouth closed.
   - **d.** Comment on the food.
2. Where will your wine glass be?
   - **a.** To the right of your plate
   - **b.** In front of your plate
   - **c.** Next to your fork
   - **d.** Behind your plate
3. What should you do if you need to make a call?
   - **a.** Talk quietly.
   - **b.** Leave the table.
   - **c.** Apologize to the other diners.
   - **d.** Stand behind your chair.
4. Which of the following is not covered by the rules of dining etiquette?
   - **a.** What flatware you use
   - **b.** What wine you drink
   - **c.** When you start eating
   - **d.** How you get more food
5. Which of the following is considered impolite?
   - **a.** Lifting your bowl while eating soup
   - **b.** Turning off your cell phone during dinner
   - **c.** Swallowing food before answering a question
   - **d.** Asking someone to pass you the salt

Conversation 2

Track 33 Robert, Gina, and their tour guide, Marie, are talking about differences in dining etiquette around the world. Listen to the conversation and fill in the missing words.

Gina: Marie, we noticed something strange at dinner last night. Most of the other ❶ ______ kept their fork in their left hand and their knife in their right. Was that something we should have done?

Marie: That's a cultural difference. ❷ ______ American etiquette, you should hold your fork in your right hand and ❸ ______ it to your left only when using your knife to cut something. On the other hand, Europeans use their left hand to hold the fork and their right to hold the knife.

Robert: That's another thing I should learn — cultural differences with table ❹ ______.

Marie: To become a tour guide with this company, you must pass a test about them. I learned a lot while studying for it. For example, in Asia, you mustn't point with your ❺ ______. It's ❻ ______ very rude.

Gina: In addition to that, I heard you should never eat with your left hand in the Middle East because it is believed to be unclean.

Marie: That's right. Waiters must serve food with their right hand there, and you ought to use your right hand to eat.

Robert: You mean you should keep your fork in your right hand?

Marie: Actually, there are many countries where you use your hand, not a ❼ ______, to eat.

Robert: And that's something that would be considered pretty ❽ ______ in a nice restaurant in the States.

Words to Remember

Use the words in the box to complete the sentences.

diner	*switch*	*according to*	*manners*
chopsticks	*consider*	*utensil*	*impolite*

1. ______ my travel guide, the museum should be around the corner.
2. Every night, this bar is so packed with ______.
3. In Thailand, touching the head of a child is quite ______.
4. Many Europeans have trouble eating with ______.
5. John likes Dan. He ______ him to be one of his best friends.

Get It Right

A. Read the story below about Susan's dining experience.

Last night, Susan had dinner at a restaurant. She sat down and moved her napkin onto the tablecloth. Then, she was thirsty, so she grabbed the glass to her left and drank. One of her friends called, and she chatted with him for a few minutes at the table. When the first course came, which was a salad, she used the fork closest to her plate to eat it. She used her fingers, too. No one else had their food yet, but she kept eating. Did she do anything wrong?

B. Using what you have learned about dining etiquette in this unit, write a paragraph about what Susan should (or ought to) have done instead.

Susan did several things wrong at dinner. To begin with, she should have put her napkin in her lap, not on the tablecloth. Then, ...

____

____

____

____

Grammar Bite

We use *should*, *ought*, and *must* to suggest an obligation to do something or to advise someone about something.

should	1. Used more frequently than ought 2. Past Tense = **should have + past participle** • I *should* learn more about cultural differences.
ought	1. Must use the infinitive with to before other verbs 2. Past Tense = **ought to have + past participle** • You *ought* to use your left hand to hold the fork.
must	1. Stronger than should and ought 2. Not used to show obligation in past tense • You *must* pass a test to become a tour guide for this company.

Give It a Try

Use the correct word of obligation (*should, ought,* or *must*) to complete each of the following sentences.

1. You really ______ to chew your food more slowly.
2. Everyone ______ show his or her passport to the immigration officer.
3. We ______ ask the waiter to bring us our check now.
4. I ______ have called the restaurant to make a reservation.

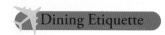

Prepare Yourself

Think about the differences in etiquette between the areas on the map. With a partner, mention any etiquette rules you know for the areas you see.

Activity 1

In which area(s) of the world is each action from the box below considered polite or OK? In which areas might it seem strange or rude?

bow when greeting someone	*tip after a meal*	*take off shoes before entering a home*
comment on someone's weight	*give a clock as a gift*	*ask someone how much he / she earns*
haggle on a price in a store	*slurp one's food*	*leave food on plate when you finish*

Activity 2

In a small group, pretend that you are introducing someone to the etiquette of your country. What actions are considered polite or rude in the following situations? Take turns asking and answering questions about the proper etiquette.

Useful Expressions

- It's polite to give a gift when *you're invited to someone's house.*
- When visiting a person's home, you should *remain standing until you're invited to sit down.*
- It's very impolite to *take your shoes off in a restaurant.*
- When you're at work, you mustn't *chat on the phone with friends.*
- In my country, you *should shake hands* when meeting someone.

Units 7-9
REVIEW 3

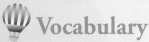

Listening

A. Track 34 Listen to the speakers and choose the best responses.

1. a. I would love to have something healthy for breakfast.
   b. Yes, that's why I always have fruit for breakfast.
   c. No, that's why I never eat anything that's greasy.
   d. I think eating healthy foods is very good for us.
2. a. It looks interesting. We should give it a try sometime.
   b. I don't feel like eating Indian food. Maybe another day.
   c. That's great! I've always wanted to go there.
   d. Well, we will be heading there in a few minutes.
3. a. Me too. I always order fish or shrimp when I eat out.
   b. Why not? You shouldn't be picky about food.
   c. Really? That's a shame because seafood tastes great.
   d. Oh, no, I didn't know you were a vegetarian.

B. Track 35 Listen to the conversation and number the events in the correct order.

_____ 1. A hotel worker collects the finished breakfast from the guest.
_____ 2. A hotel staff member introduces breakfast options.
_____ 3. The breakfast gets sent to room 821.
_____ 4. The guest places an order with the room service staff.
_____ 5. A hotel guest calls room service to order breakfast.

Vocabulary

Circle the the word that does not fit the group.

1.	sunny side up	over easy	scrambled	overcook
2.	chopsticks	dinner fork	salad plate	dessert fork
3.	bistro	restaurant	diner	teppanyaki
4.	flute	goblet	bowl	glass
5.	baked beans	congee	hash browns	croissants
6.	sushi bar	lobster	milkshake	seafood restaurant

Grammar

Choose the correct sentence.

1. **a.** I will have leave the country by this time tomorrow.
   b. I will have left the country by this time tomorrow.
2. **a.** You ought to mind your table manners when eating.
   b. You should minded your table manners when eating.
3. **a.** If you finish your food, I may give you some dessert.
   b. If you finished your food, I may give to you some dessert.

Reading

Complete the words in the text. The first letters are given.

October 26, 2013
Saturday

I accompanied my boss to a fancy restaurant to meet with a cl__________, Mr. Wu. I have to say, I've never experienced anything quite as interesting before.

The food was delicious, you can tell that everything was made from fresh, hi__________ ingredients. Well, they have to be because of the ridiculously expensive menu. I wouldn't have had the chance to try it if I wasn't on this bus__________ trip. I had my first taste of champagne, too. Honestly, I did not like it, but I had to pretend because Mr. Wu bought it for the table. Oh, and the des__________ was to die for. I ordered a simple brownie with vanilla ice cream, and it was the best I've had my whole life.

The most mem__________ thing for me though, was the large range of tab__________ that was in front of me. I had no idea what I was supposed to do with any of them! Luckily, Mr. Wu was very kind to give me a few simple tips:

- Eat to the left and drink to the right.
- Start with the cutlery farthest from the plate and work my way in, using one ute__________ for each course.
- Cutlery must never touch the table again after being used; always rest them on the side of the plate.

Thanks to Mr. Wu, I was able to get through dinner without off__________ anyone, although I was extremely nervous the whole time. He also told me what everything was for, but I doubt I'll ever remember. Truthfully, I don't need to. I probably won't use them again. Dining at fancy restaurants is great, but how can you enjoy a meal with so many rules?

Unit 10

Getting on a Train

By the end of this unit, you will be able to do the following:

- Buy a train ticket
- Find your way around a train station
- Use acronyms
- Understand train tickets

Before We Go

Train stations can be busy and confusing places. To help yourself find your way around one, take a look at the pictures and list of vocabulary below. Use the terms to label the pictures.

platform	*ticket barrier*	*information*	*ticket counter*
conductor	*tracks*	*timetable*	*train carriage*

❶ ____________

❷ ____________

❸ ____________

❹ ____________

❺ ____________

❻ ____________

❼ ____________

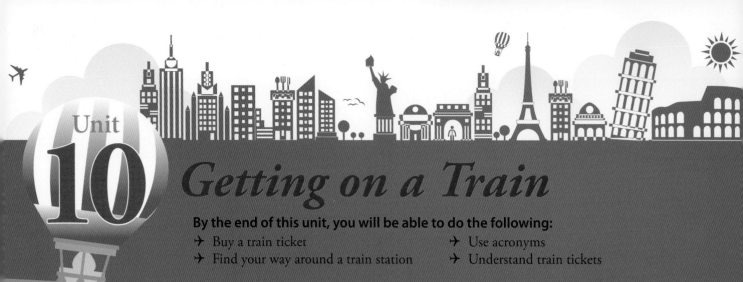

❽ ____________

Useful Expressions

- I prefer traveling by *train* to traveling by *bus* because *you can't get stuck in traffic jams.*
- The worst train ride I've ever had was in *Macedonia* when *a policeman pointed a gun at me and asked for my passport.*
- I usually *read* when I'm on the train.
- My best train experience came in France as *the train was so fast and clean.*

Conversation 1

Track 36 Tony is at the train station buying a ticket for a trip to New York. Listen to the conversation and fill in the missing words.

Tony: Hi, there. I'd like to get a ticket for New York, please.

Ticket seller: Are you planning to travel today?

Tony: Yes, I'd like to go as soon as possible.

Ticket seller: OK, do you want a ❶ __________ or a ❷ __________ ticket?

Tony: A single, please.

Ticket seller: Do you have student ❸ __________ or any ❹ __________?

Tony: No, I'm a bit too old to be a student, and I didn't know I could get a railcard.

Ticket seller: If you're going to be traveling a lot, you might want to consider ❺ __________ the USA Rail ❻ __________. The 15-day pass only costs $389, and you can you use it for free travel on almost all of our services.

Tony: I wish I had known about that at the beginning of my vacation. It would have saved me a lot of money.

Ticket seller: Oh well, maybe next time. Anyway, in terms of your journey today, there are two trains you might want to take. There's a regular service which ❼ __________ in 20 minutes and will arrive at 3:15 this afternoon, or there's an ❽ __________ train which will get you there at 2:30, but it doesn't set off for another hour and a half.

Tony: How much do they cost?

Ticket seller: The express is $80 and the regular train is $55.

Tony: I'll ❾ __________ the regular train. I can take a ❿ __________ on the journey.

Ticket seller: Right, well, that'll be $55 then, please.

Words to Remember

Choose the words in the box to complete the passage.

go for	*return*	*purchase*	*express*	*single*
pass	*ID*	*depart*	*railcard*	*nap*

Tina packed her bag and got everything ready for her train journey, but since her train was not going to ❶ __________ for another three hours, she decided to go to bed. When she woke up from her ❷ __________, however, she only had 30 minutes to get to the station and buy her ticket. She went to the ticket counter and got a ticket for the ❸ __________ train. She was able to get a discount as she has a ❹ __________. Before she got on the train, she had time to ❺ __________ a snack for her journey.

Reading

Track 37 **Train operators often provide passengers with a list of safety instructions. Look at the example printed below, and check any words you do not know.**

If there is an emergency, use the emergency intercom (next to the door) to talk to the driver and train conductor. Using the intercom if there isn't an emergency will result in a fine.

Fire

- If there is a fire, move quickly and calmly to another carriage.
- Follow the instructions given by the train conductor and emergency workers.
- Do not leave the train unless you are told to.

Medical emergencies

- If you see a passenger suffering with a medical emergency, tell the conductor immediately.
- If you are medically qualified to help, tell the conductor who you are.

Criminal activity

- If you see a passenger behaving suspiciously or aggressively, tell the conductor. He or she will contact the police.

Evacuation

- If you are told to leave the train, open the emergency box next to the door and pull the handle.
- If this does not open the door, use the emergency hammer to break a window.

Luggage

- Do not put any bags in the aisle. Instead, put them in the luggage areas next to the doors or under your legs.
- Make sure you take all your possessions when you leave the train.

Getting off

- Exit carefully, and mind the gap between the train and the platform.

Give It a Try

Read the information again and choose the best responses to each of the following questions.

1. What will happen if you use the emergency intercom in a normal situation?
- **a.** You will be arrested.
- **b.** The train will stop.
- **c.** You will have to pay money.
- **d.** The conductor will call the police.

2. What is NOT said to be next to the doors?
- **a.** The emergency hammer
- **b.** The emergency intercom
- **c.** The emergency box
- **d.** The luggage area

3. What is the first thing you should do if there's a fire in your carriage?
- **a.** Use the emergency intercom.
- **b.** Leave the train.
- **c.** Break the windows.
- **d.** Move to a safe place.

4. What should a doctor do first if there is a medical emergency?
- **a.** Call an ambulance.
- **b.** Speak to the conductor.
- **c.** Treat the passenger.
- **d.** Ask for help.

5. What should passengers do before leaving the train?
- **a.** Open the emergency box.
- **b.** Thank the conductor.
- **c.** Take everything that belongs to them.
- **d.** Ask about the gap.

Conversation 2

Track 38 Tony has his ticket, but he can't find his way to the platform. Listen to the conversation and fill in the missing words.

Tony: Excuse me, I've just bought a ticket to New York, but I'm not sure which platform it's leaving from.

Guard: Can I take a look at your ticket?

Tony: Yeah, sure. Here it is.

Guard: Well, your departure time is 9:15, so you must be on train no. 129. It'll be ❶ ______ from platform five. The train can't have even arrived yet, so you wouldn't be able to ❷ ______ now anyway.

Tony: Thanks. I don't really have much time, and I was starting to worry that I'd miss it.

Guard: Relax, you've got plenty of time to get there.

Tony: Before you go, how exactly do I get there?

Guard: Oh, it couldn't be easier. Go up that ❸ ______ of stairs, the ones nest to the café, turn right when you get to the top, and walk along the ❹ ______ until you see the signs for the platform.

Tony: That seems ❺ ______. I wonder if I've got time to get a coffee and a snack in the café.

Guard: I wouldn't ❻ ______ it if I were you; the service in there isn't that fast. Anyway, there's a buffet car on the train, so you can get something to eat once you've found your seat. I can see a train ❼ ______ now; it might be yours.

Tony: I'd better go, then. Thanks so much for your help.

Guard: ❽ ______. Have a safe journey.

Words to Remember

Choose the words in the box to complete the following sentences.

straightforward	*risk*	*not at all*	*set off*
footbridge	*flight*	*approach*	*board*

1. I usually buy a drink and a sandwich before I ______ a train or coach.
2. A: Thank you for helping out today. **B:** ______; it was my pleasure.
3. The elevator isn't working so I had to come walk up ten ______ of stairs to get to my apartment.
4. Walking across the road is a little dangerous, so you might want to use the ______.
5. I don't want to ______ being late, so I'm going to go there now.

Get It Right

A. The evening after arriving in New York, Tony writes in his diary about his experiences. Read the passage below.

Today was an interesting day as I had to take the train to New York. It wasn't the first train ride I've taken in the U.S., but it was easily the longest. I had a little trouble buying my ticket and finding the train, but I got a lot of help from the ticket seller and guard. They must have had a lot of experience helping confused tourists like me. I also had problems when I got on the train, and I can't have sat on the right seat because an angry man told me that it was his. When I had moved and sat down again, I started eating my lunch, but I may have eaten too much because I started to feel a bit sick. Anyway, after that, I must have fallen asleep because the next thing I can remember is the train arriving in New York!

B. Now, write one of your own about a journey you have taken.

Grammar Bite

Modals of deduction are used when you can work out that something *must*, *might*, or *can't* be true.

1. **Must**

   You can use *must* when you're sure something is true.

   - I can't see her anywhere. She *must* have gone home already.

2. **Might / may / could**

   Might, *may* or *could* can be used when you think something might be true.

   - I saw some people outside that house today. They *might* have moved in.

3. **Can't / mustn't**

   When you're sure something isn't true, you can use *can't* or *mustn't*.

   - He *can't* have been shopping yet. He hasn't had enough time.

Give It a Try

Circle the correct word to complete each sentence.

1. She ***(must / may / can't)*** have eaten anything. Her lunch box is still in the fridge.
2. Their car's still in front of their house, so they ***(mustn't / must / might)*** be at home.
3. Ted's story doesn't make sense. He ***(mustn't / might / must)*** be lying.
4. Rachel didn't arrive on the train, but she ***(could / can't / must)*** have taken a bus.
5. My teacher knew all about the movie. She ***(mustn't / may / must)*** have seen it.

Prepare Yourself

Train tickets often contain a lot of information. Look at the one printed below; can you understand what's written on it?

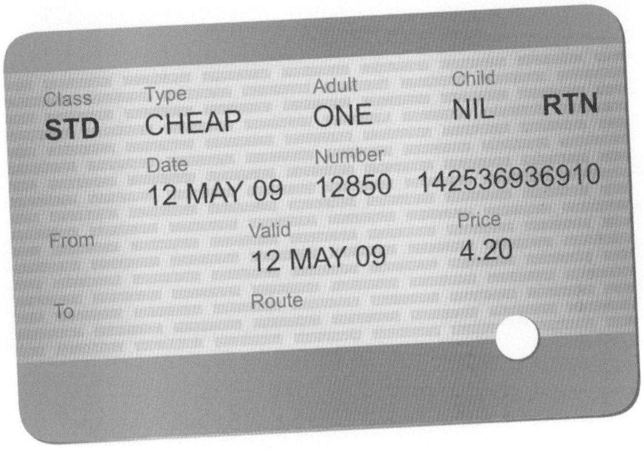

Activity 1

Talk to your partner about the ticket and what each piece of information means. For example, where is the traveler going, how much did they pay for the ticket, and is it a single or a return?

Activity 2

Look at the diagram of a train below. With a partner, take turns pretending to be a passenger asking for information about where they can find their seat or some kind of service on the train.

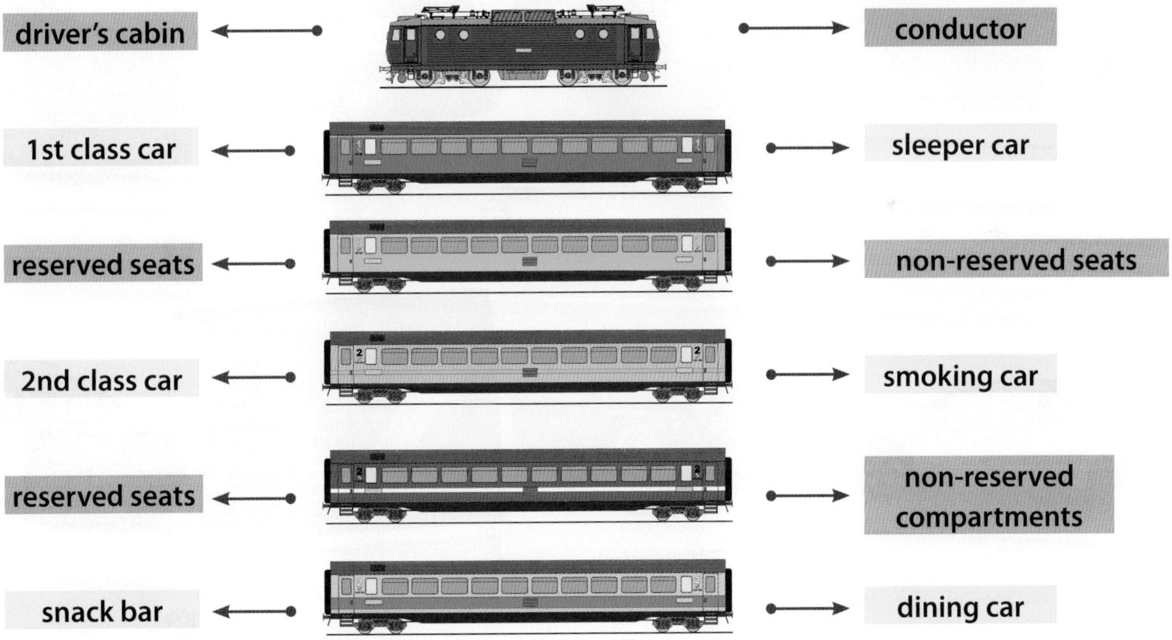

Useful Expressions

- Can you tell me where I can find *the first-class area*?
- It's at the *back* of the train in *carriage nine*.
- There are a few *toilets* on the train. There's one *toilet* area at the *end of each carriage*.
- *Carriage five* is right in the middle of the train.

Unit 11

Car Rentals

By the end of this unit, you will be able to do the following:

- Identify different types of car
- Describe a driving experience
- Ask for and give advice about cars
- Use relative clauses to create more informative sentences

Before We Go

Before you rent a car, you have to decide what kind of vehicle you want to drive. Take a look at the pictures of different cars below and use the terms from the box to label them.

sedan	*hatchback*	*convertible*	*automatic*
coupe	*SUV*	*minivan*	*stick shift*

❶ ____________

❷ ____________

❸ ____________

❹ ____________

❺ ____________

❻ ____________

❼ ____________

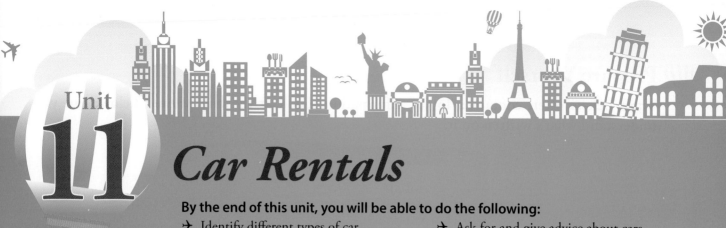

❽ ____________

Useful Expressions

- I usually drive *automatic* cars because *they're not as difficult to control.*
- If you're with a lot of people, a *minivan* might be useful.
- If I rent a car on my next vacation I'll get a *convertible* so *I can put down the roof and feel the wind in my hair.*
- I think we all need to *do more to look after the environment,* so I want to drive a hybrid.

Conversation 1

Track 39 Joanne is at a car rental office to get a vehicle for her vacation. Listen to the conversation and fill in the missing words.

Joanne: I'd like to rent a car for four days. How much will that cost me?

Dealer: That ❶ ________ on what kind of car you rent. Is there anything in ❷ ________ you'd like?

Joanne: I'd prefer to get a hybrid if it's possible.

Dealer: It is. We have several ❸ ________ hybrids, but they are about 50% more expensive than a standard-size sedan.

Joanne: That's OK. I don't mind paying a little extra to help the ❹ ________.

Dealer: Would you be the only person driving the car?

Joanne: Yes, just me. ❺ ________, I'll give you my driver's license.

Dealer: Thanks, I'll get a copy of this. Would you write your contact details on this ❻ ________ please? Would you like to pay for ❼ ________? It'll cost you $50 per day, but you'll be protected if your vehicle is damaged in any way.

Joanne: Yes, I suppose that would be good idea. Listen, I was just thinking that it might be more convenient for me to return the car to your ❽ ________ in Atlanta. Is that OK?

Dealer: Yes. You can return it to any one of our offices around the country. When you're ready, I'll take you outside so you can check the car for existing ❾ ________ and scratches.

Joanne: OK, I'm ready now.

Dealer: Excellent. I'll just get the ❿ ________.

Words to Remember

Choose the words in the box to complete the sentences.

dent	*mid-size*	*paperwork*	*branch office*	*insurance*
form	*particular*	*depend*	*hold on*	*environment*

1. Gary doesn't work at the company's headquarters. He's the manager of a ________.
2. Many scientists believe that global warming is damaging the ________.

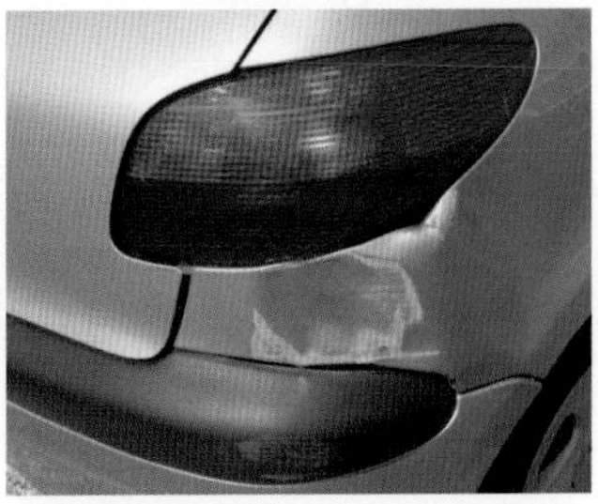

3. There is a ________ in Mike's car from where he drove into a wall.
4. Dawn has a lot of ________ to finish before she can go home.
5. ________, don't go yet! I'll be finished soon.

Reading

Track 40 **While most people rent cars in order to get somewhere, some just like to go on beautiful drives when they're on vacation. Read this passage about a beautiful drive in Italy.**

Drive the Amalfi Coast

The roads that wind their way down Italy's Amalfi Coast make for one of the most beautiful drives in the world. Not only is the scenery stunningly beautiful, but the narrow road's many twists and turns mean that driving along them is an exciting, sometimes terrifying, but always pleasurable experience.

From Sorrento down to Salerno, the roads stay close to the Mediterranean Sea – although they do sometimes head inland. On one side of you, steep cliffs fall away to the sparkling green and blue waters below, while on the other side, green hillsides rise steeply into the Southern European skies.

At regular intervals along your journey, you'll pass by charming old towns and villages that seem to have been carved out of the hillsides around them. The pink, white, blue, and brown buildings, their colors made lighter by the burning Mediterranean sun, are often built around a beautiful old church. When you want a break from the road, any one of these towns would be worth exploring.

The locals say the best time to drive here is in the spring and fall when there are fewer tour buses on the roads. However, you still need to watch out for young Italian drivers, who like to test their bravery by driving their cars as fast as they can.

Whenever you go, however, you're sure to have an experience you'll remember forever.

Give It a Try

Read the passage again and choose the best responses to each of the following questions.

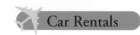

1. What is said about the towns and villages?
   a. They all contain a church.
   b. They're all interesting.
   c. Many are built at the bottom of the cliffs.
   d. They are mostly difficult to explore.
2. Why wouldn't you drive along the Amalfi Coast in the summer?
   a. Because it's too hot.
   b. Because of all the young Italians.
   c. Because there are lots of big vehicles.
   d. Because the scenery looks bad at that time.
3. What color of building is NOT mentioned in the passage?
   a. Green
   b. Blue
   c. Brown
   d. White
4. What does the writer say about driving down the Amalfi coast?
   a. It can be a scary experience.
   b. It's the best drive in the world.
   c. You will want to take a break from it.
   d. It is an easy thing to do.
5. What do you know about the roads?
   a. They're easy to get lost on.
   b. They're mostly steep.
   c. They're all very old.
   d. They're not always next to the sea.

Conversation 2

Track 41 Joanne returns her car to the office in Atlanta. Listen to the conversation and fill in the missing words.

Dealer: Good afternoon, ma'am. Are you here to return a car?

Joanne: Yes, it's the blue hybrid outside. I rented it from your branch in Phoenix.

Dealer: Have you had any problems with the car?

Joanne: I had a devil of a time ❶ ______ the driver's seat; I think that might need to be fixed, but there were no serious issues.

Dealer: OK, I'll get someone to look at that. Are there any new dents or scratches that we should know about?

Joanne: There is a scratch on the ❷ ______ door, which happened when a cyclist ❸ ______ into me.

Dealer: OK, I'll check that in a minute. Did you have insurance?

Joanne: Yes, ❹ ______! ❺ ______ I'd be paying through the nose in fines.

Dealer: Well, we do advise everyone to pay for insurance. We find that it gives people ❻ ______. Is there any other damage to the vehicle?

Joanne: There is a mark on the ❼ ______ which was there when I ❽ ______ the car. The man who sorted out the rental agreement for me made a note of it on the paperwork. I don't think there's anything else.

Dealer: OK, can I take a look at the rental agreement forms? And could I see your driver's license as well?

Joanne: Yes, of course. Oh, silly me; I left them in the ❾ ______ ❿ ______. Let me go and dig them out for you.

Words to Remember

Use the words in the box to complete the sentences.

otherwise	*passenger*	*trunk*	*peace of mind*	*glove*
compartment	*bump*	*lease*	*thank goodness*	*adjust*

1. I expected Dan to be driving, so I was surprised to see him in the ______ seat.
2. Put your suitcase in the ______; there isn't enough room for it in the back of the car.
3. Cathy's going overseas for a year, so she wants to ______ out her apartment.
4. Go to sleep early; ______ you'll feel tired tomorrow.
5. ______ it's going to be sunny tomorrow! I don't want to be stuck in the house again.

Get It Right

A. Read the following passage about a drive in England.

In England, some of the best scenery can be found in Herefordshire, which is in the west of the country. There is a beautiful drive from Hereford to a little town called Ross-on-Wye, where you'll find a gorgeous old church. Although you will pass some small villages on the journey, the road mostly takes you through the English countryside, which is famous for its green hills and pretty fields. Farmers in this part of the country keep sheep and cows, and many of them also grow apples, which are used to make delicious cider. The best time to do this drive is in the fall, which is called "autumn" in England. At this time of the year, the leaves on the trees will be turning orange, brown, and red, and the colors make the scenery even nicer. Also, the farmers who produce apples might sell you some of their fruits for very low prices.

B. Introduce a great drive from somewhere in your country. Include details about where the drive starts and ends, what kind of scenery you can see, what time of year is best to do the drive, and other information you can think of.

Grammar Bite

Relative clauses are used to give more information about a person, place, or thing in a sentence.

1. Defining clauses	2. Non-defining clauses
Defining clauses are used to give essential information and they don't need commas. **who → people** • The woman *who* you spoke to earlier is my sister. **which / that → things** • The book *that* you gave me yesterday is boring. **where → places** • The restaurant *where* we ate has closed down.	The clauses are used to give additional information and they usually have commas. **who – people** • This is Tom, *who* I met on vacation. **which – things** • This movie, *which* was made ten years ago, is great. **where – places** • Fifi's Café, *where* I often relax, is looking for new staff.

Give It a Try

Decide whether these sentences contain defining or non-defining relative clauses. Add commas if you think they're non-defining relative clauses.

1. My new teacher, who I really like, is called Ms. Michaels.
2. The town where I grew up is in the countryside.
3. This pen which I borrowed from Amy has stopped working.
4. My best friend who I've known for 20 years is moving to another country.
5. The hotel that my mother works in has great deals on rooms next month.

Prepare Yourself

Have a look at the following car rental company advertisements. What other offers do you think companies might make in order to attract customers?

- *Return your car to any of our offices*
- *Low-cost insurance*
- *We have a wide range of cars to choose from*
- *Every car is provided with a full tank of gas*
- *Fast service*
- *No daily driving limits*

Activity 1

Talk to your partner about the advertisements. What things would be most important to you if you were renting a car?

Activity 2

Each of the three people shown below wants to rent a car. Read the information about them and talk to your partner about what kind of vehicle would be best for them.

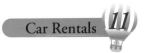

Kevin
- Traveling with his wife and two children
- Needs room for suitcases and toys
- Traveling on a budget

Winnie
- Driving on her own down the Amalfi Coast in summer
- Not an experienced driver and wants something easy to drive

Eva
- Driving her supervisor and company CEO from the airport to a business conference
- Money is not important, but comfort for her passengers is
- Her passengers also want to do some work on the journey

Useful Expressions

- I would advise *Kevin* to get a *minivan* because *they have the most room?*
- I disagree. I think *Kevin* would be better off in *a standard-size sedan* because *he doesn't have much money.*
- Winnie doesn't need *a big car*, so I would rent a *compact* if I were *her.*

Unit 12

Taking a Cruise

By the end of this unit, you will be able to do the following:

- Find your way around a ship
- Weigh up both sides of an argument
- Use prefixes to make negative sentences
- Make comparisons

Before We Go

Modern cruise ships are huge with many different rooms, decks, and items. Take a look at the terms below and try to match them to the pictures.

bow	*port*	*deck*	*galley*	*cabin*
stern	*starboard*	*bridge*	*gangplank*	*lifeboat*

1. ____________
2. ____________
3. ____________
4. ____________
5. ____________
6. ____________
7. ____________

8. ____________

9. ____________

10. ____________

Useful Expressions

- I have never taken a cruise; *they seem to be very expensive.*
- I went on a cruise *once* and *had a great time.*
- I would love to go on a cruise because *it's a great way to relax and see lots of different places.*
- I'm not interested in taking a cruise because *I think I would get bored.*

Conversation 1

Track 42 Keith asks his travel agent about different types of cruises. Listen to the conversation and fill in the missing words.

Keith: My wife's really interested in taking a cruise, so I want to ask what different ❶ ______ there are.

Travel agent: ❷ ______, cruises are quite ❸ ______, and passengers ❹ ______ for dinner, but there are quite a few more relaxed cruises now.

Keith: What else can you tell me about cruises; I really have no idea about them.

Travel agent: On many cruises, you have dinner at the same time every day, and you sit at the same table with the same people.

Keith: I'm not sure I like the sound of that.

Travel agent: Not everyone does. It depends on people's ❺ ______. The good news for you is that many companies are now operating "❻ ______" cruises. If you go on one of those, you'll be able to eat whenever you want, and you can choose whether to dine alone or on a large table with other passengers.

Keith: That sounds quite ❼ ______.

Travel agent: It's still possible to dress up for dinner if you want, and many of my ❽ ______ say they enjoy putting on ❾ ______ and ❿ ______ for a couple of evenings.

Keith: How much do freestyle cruises usually cost?

Travel agent: They're usually cheaper than the more traditional options.

Keith: So why would anyone choose a formal cruise?

Travel agent: As I say, it depends on a passenger's personality. Also, there are always more families on freestyle cruises, and not everyone likes that.

Keith: Ah, OK. Well, thanks for the information. I'll talk about it with my wife.

Words to Remember

Use the words in the box to complete the sentences.

formal	*client*	*freestyle*	*personality*	*appealing*
tuxedo	*option*	*dress up*	*ball gown*	*traditionally*

1. You can't wear shorts to the dinner; you should ______.
2. Eric is one of my ______. I manage all of his business affairs.
3. I love curry, so an invitation to an Indian restaurant is very ______.
4. Christmas is ______ a time for families.
5. The women at the dinner party all looked beautiful in long ______.

Reading

Track 43 **Cruises were not traditionally thought of as family vacations, but some companies are now trying to change that by offering more children's activities and family-themed events. Read the information about a family cruise below.**

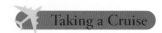

Magic Cruises are perfect for family vacations

At Magic Cruises, we believe that family vacations are important, and we do everything possible to make sure that parents and children have a great time on our ships. Our staff members are friendly, patient, and trained to deal with children, and our ships have been designed with families in mind. The cabins are large, with a separate bedroom for mom and dad and a lounge area that can easily be converted into a bedroom for the children.

There are a range of clubs for children of different ages, and there are fun activities for them to do every day. There are also basketball courts, reading rooms, and movie theaters on board where the whole family can enjoy the latest movies together. Our ships each have two family pools with water slides and fun toys. There are also separate, adult-only pool areas where grown-ups can relax and spend some time away from their children.

We stop at a wide variety of locations, but we always keep families in mind. Some of our ports are historic towns and old streets and interesting stores, and others are near beautiful beaches. If you don't want to get off the ship, you can always stay on board and enjoy the pools and games areas.

For more information about prices and routes, please visit our Web site. Discounts are available for people booking more than a year in advance and for those who have sailed with us before.

Give It a Try

Read the passage again and choose the best responses to each of the following questions.

1. What should people do if they want more information about the cruises?
   a. Call Magic Cruises. **c.** Go on the Internet.
   b. Talk to a travel agent. **d.** Write an e-mail.
2. What kind of leisure area is NOT mentioned in the passage?
   a. Games rooms **c.** Tennis courts
   b. Theaters **d.** Reading areas
3. Where can parents go to spend time away from their children?
   a. Beaches **c.** A pool
   b. Historic towns **d.** Living rooms
4. How many pools are there on the ships?
   a. One **c.** Three
   b. Two **d.** Four
5. What do you know about the cruises?
   a. First-time passengers pay more. **c.** Only families are allowed to go on them.
   b. Passengers have to book their tickets early. **d.** They are quite new services.

Conversation 2

Track 44 **Keith and his wife, Michelle, talk about cruises, and where they would like to go. Listen to the conversation and fill in the missing words.**

Michelle: So, are you sure you want to go on a cruise? Whenever I've said it would be a good idea, you've always disagreed.

Keith: I know, and if the travel agent hadn't told me about freestyle cruises, I would still be ❶ ______.

Michelle: I must thank her. I'm so happy you've had a ❷ ______.

Keith: Me too. Now we just have to decide on where we want to go.

Michelle: I think it would be great to sail around the world, just stopping at a few major ports along the way.

Keith: No, spending so many days at sea would drive me ❸ ______. Just the ❹ ______ of it sends ❺ ______ down my spine!

Michelle: But your brother went on a round-the-world cruise last year, and he loved it.

Keith: If he had gone with me, he wouldn't be saying he had a great time. Trust me, I won't be good ❻ ______ when our ship's in the middle of the ❼ ______.

Michelle: So what do you suggest?

Keith: I was thinking about a Mediterranean cruise. We can still enjoy all the facilities on the ship, but we'll also be able to ❽ ______ regularly and see some beautiful European cities.

Michelle: That's not a bad idea. How much would a trip like that cost?

Keith: No idea. I'll call the travel agent and ask.

Words to Remember

Use the words in the box to complete the passage below.

shiver	*company*	*disembark*	*change of heart*
insane	*prospect*	*unenthusiastic*	*Pacific Ocean*

I used to think Tony was ❶ ______ because his opinions often seem strange, but I've had a ❷ ______ recently and I now think he's very nice and thoughtful. About a year ago, I was always ❸ ______ about spending time with him, but I now enjoy his ❹ ______. The ❺ ______ of meeting him tomorrow makes me feel really happy.

Get It Right

A. Read the following passage about a cruise. Familiarize yourself with the writing style.

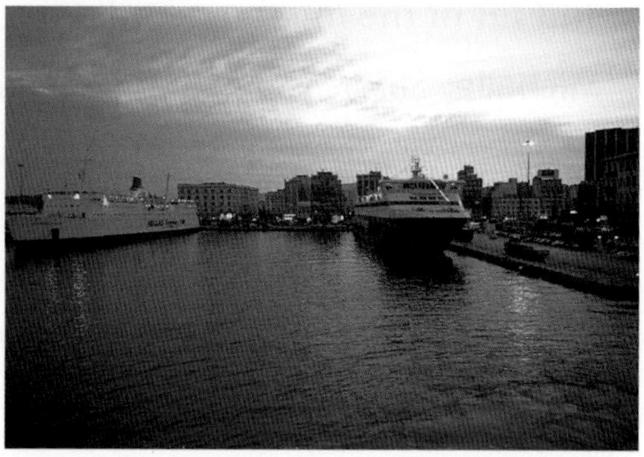

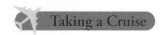

I know that cruise ships are very safe, but I can't swim and am afraid of water, so I would feel scared if I had to take a vacation on one. I know that cruises are also quite expensive, even if you go on a modern, freestyle cruise, and I don't make a lot of money in my job.

I have heard that cruise ships are very beautiful and that the bedrooms are very comfortable and relaxing, and that sounds great. There are also usually lots of things you can do fun on board. For example, many ships have theaters, pools, games rooms, and casinos.

I think I probably won't ever go on a cruise. I know they can be good vacations, but I would prefer to use my money for something else. If I had met someone who had always dreamed of going on a cruise, though, I would change my mind.

B. What are the positive and negative aspects of taking a cruise? Write about both, and then say whether you would like to go on a cruise and why. Try to use mixed second and third conditionals in your passage.

Grammar Bite

The second conditional refers to hopes and dreams. It deals with what would happen if something were true. The third conditional refers to the past. It deals with what would have happened if something else had happened. In English, it is possible to combine the second and third conditional to talk about what would happen if something else had happened.

Third conditional past action	Second conditional present result
• If she had taken her medicine,	she would feel better now.
• If we had left the house earlier,	we would be there already.
• If I hadn't taken my books home,	I would still be writing my homework.
• If they hadn't read the book,	they wouldn't know how to write the assignment.

Give It a Try

Rewrite these sentences using mixed second and third conditionals.

1. They played tennis all day. They are tired.

____

2. I didn't eat dinner. I feel hungry.

____

3. He bought a new computer. He has no money.

____

4. My sister ate lots of chocolate. She feels sick.

____

5. The café lowered its prices. It is very busy.

____

Prepare Yourself

Where would you want to go on a cruise? Would you like to relax on sandy beaches, visit historic European towns, go sightseeing across Asia, or check out the Middle East? Take a look at the map below and think about what you'd find in each place.

Activity 1

In a small group, talk about where you would like to go on a cruise. Explain why you want to go there and what you would want to see and do.

Activity 2

Take a look at the information below about two very different cruise lines. Which one would you be more interested in? What kind of person do you think would like a cruise on the other service?

At Royal Oriental, we like to remember the golden age of cruising, when people dressed for dinner and traveled in complete luxury. We operate smaller ships, meaning that we can offer all of our passengers a very personal service. Every cabin has been carefully decorated to ensure that wherever you stay, you will be able to relax in comfort.

Our three dining rooms offer different menus, but guests will be expected to dine in formal, evening wear. In addition to the restaurants, our ships have ball rooms, casinos, bars, and pools.

Let your dreams set sail on a Royal Caribbean cruise.

Playtime Cruises operate the most entertaining, relaxing, and enjoyable cruises in the world. There are no rules about what to wear for dinner or what time you have to eat. If you feel hungry, make your way to one of the ship's many restaurants and place an order.

Our ships are some of the biggest sailing the seas, and that means we can provide you with more facilities. We have pools, water slides, movie theaters, snack bars, basketball courts, pool halls, and even relaxation rooms for when you just want to sit quietly.

Our passengers keep coming back and booking again. Why not find out why they love us so much!

Useful Expressions

- I'm more interested in *Royal Oriental cruises* because *I want luxury and a high-class vacation.*
- I think *Playtime Cruises* might be fun, but *there might be too much noise and excitement.*
- I think *older* people would be interested in *Royal Oriental.*
- My guess is that *young families* would get more enjoyment from *Playtime Cruises.*

Units 10-12
REVIEW 4

Listing

A. Track 45 **Listen to the speakers and choose the best responses.**

1. **a.** No, I can't give you any advice on which car to rent.
   b. Yes, I usually go for SUVs because I have a big family.
   c. Yes, I would advise you rent a car on this trip.
   d. No, I think renting a car is better than driving your own.
2. **a.** You can probably get one at the ticket counter.
   b. I'm sorry, I don't know what the time is.
   c. Yes, I had time to take a train trip last year.
   d. I'm not sure, maybe we can find out on the train.
3. **a.** Yes, I went on a cruise last year and had a terrible time.
   b. I'm more interested in a cruise because it sounds like fun.
   c. No, I'm not interested. They are way too expensive.
   d. Well, I think older people would like cruises more.

B. Track 46 **Listen to the short talk and choose the correct statements.**

☐ **1.** The minivan is the best choice if you want something sporty.
☐ **2.** The car rental company offers numerous types of vehicles.
☐ **3.** Only the hybrid will allow you to save on fuel.
☐ **4.** No-smoking vehicles will only be provided upon request.
☐ **5.** The SUV or minivan will be suitable for bigger families.
☐ **6.** This car rental company is based in the United States.

C. Track 47 **Listen to the conversation and choose the best answer to each question.**

1. Where did this conversation take place?
   a. On the train
   b. By the ticket counter
   c. On the platform
   d. By the tracks
2. Which of the following is not true?
   a. The man checked the woman's ticket.
   b. The woman bought some snacks.
   c. There won't be any delay in arrival.
   d. The food will be cheaper for passengers.

Vocabulary

Match the vocabulary to its correct definition.

_____ **1.** depart
_____ **2.** trunk
_____ **3.** pass
_____ **4.** port
_____ **5.** hybrid
_____ **6.** disembark

a. a permission or license to pass, go, come, or enter
b. a vehicle that is powered by more than one power source
c. to go away or leave
d. to leave a ship or vehicle
e. a large compartment in the back of a car
f. a place along the coast where ships can load or unload

Grammar

Choose the correct sentence.

1. **a.** If she had prepared for the speech, she wouldn't feel embarrassed now.
b. If she had prepared for the speech, she will feel embarrassed now.

2. **a.** The house is quiet. My family must have gone out for dinner.
b. The house is quiet. My family must go out for dinner.

3. **a.** The woman, who prepared the roast chicken is my sister.
b. The woman who prepared the roast chicken is my sister.

4. **a.** They can't be on holiday yet. The kids must be at school.
b. They can't have been on holiday yet. The kids are still in school.

5. **a.** If we had left the hotel later, we wouldn't watch the movie.
b. If we had left the hotel later, we would be watching the movie.

6. **a.** The new car, which is dark red, is a present from my parents.
b. The new car which is dark red is a present from my parents.

Unit 13

In a Department Store

By the end of this unit, you will be able to do the following:

- Ask for clothes in different colors and sizes
- Ask for and give directions around a department store

Before We Go

Department stores are usually large places with many different floors and sections. Look at the list of departments written below and use them to label the pictures.

food court	*cosmetics*	*home appliances*	*designer boutique*
jewelry	*sportswear*	*home furnishing*	*formal wear*

❶ ______

❷ ______

❸ ______

❹ ______

❺ ______

❻ ______

❼ ______

❽ ______

Useful Expressions

- I don't go to *department stores* very often. I think they're *too expensive*.
- The first place I usually go in a department store is the *sportswear* department.
- I usually buy *casual* clothing.
- I spend most money in the *home furnishings* department.

Conversation 1

Track 48 **Beth is having trouble finding her way around a large department store, so she asks a clerk for directions. Listen to the conversation and fill in the missing words.**

Beth: Excuse me, does this store have a sportswear department? I really want to get myself a ❶ ______.

Clerk: Yes, you'll find a few sportswear outlets on the eighth floor; they're right next to the ❷ ______ section.

Beth: OK, I guess I'd better find an ❸ ______ to get myself up there.

Clerk: You'll find them on your left, and if they're busy, you can take an ❹ ______. They're located in the center of each floor.

Beth: That's wonderful. Do you know if there's an ATM up on the eighth floor? I need to take some cash out.

Clerk: I actually don't know; I don't really go up there much. There are definitely a couple of machines on the ❺ ______. Take the escalator down and walk through the cosmetics department. You'll see the ATMs on the right.

Beth: That's ❻ ______; I was thinking about buying a new ❼ ______ as well.

Clerk: Today's a good day to buy one. They're having a ❽ ______ down there.

Beth: That sounds great. You've been a big help. Thank you so much for your kindness.

Clerk: Don't mention it. It's just part of the job. Have a good day shopping, and if you need a pair of sunglasses, please come back. I'll be more than happy to show you our ❾ ______.

Beth: Thanks, maybe I will.

Words to Remember

Use the words in the box to complete the sentences.

elevator	*lipstick*	*promotion*	*selection*	*ground floor*
escalator	*hoodie*	*maternity*	*handy*	

1. The store's having a big ______, so everything is 25% off.
2. There's a convenience store right next to my apartment building, which is very ______.
3. This store has a great ______ of books. There are many different kinds of things here.
4. I love wearing my ______ because it's so warm and comfortable.
5. You should be careful if you get on an ______ while wearing rubber shoes.

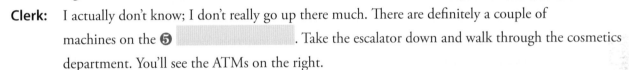

Reading

Track 49 Department stores sell different kinds of clothes to appeal to different kinds of people. Read the information below about a new range of clothing. Would you be interested in buying anything from this collection?

Sloan's

Sloan's is a new, high-class range of clothing that will only be sold in Sugu department stores across Asia. Every item in the collection has been carefully designed with style and comfort in mind, and these pieces will make you feel good about yourself.

The Sloan's range includes clothes for men, women, children, and babies. There are pieces you can wear for business meetings, formal dinners, yacht parties, and lazy afternoons at home. It is our intention that you can buy everything you'll ever need to wear from our collection. And if you do, you'll always be able to take simple, elegant clothes from your closet.

All of our clothes are made from the very best natural materials. We use 100% Egyptian cotton in many of our items, including T-shirts, shirts, suits, and pants. For our silk blouses, we take only the finest silk, and our sweaters are always made with pure lamb's wool.

The clothes will go on sale in China and Hong Kong in September this year and will be in stores across the rest of the continent three months later. To have a look at what we have to offer and to make an early order, visit our Web site at www.sloansclothes.com.

Give It a Try

Read the passage again and choose the best responses to each of the following questions.

1. What are Sloan's suits made from?
- **a.** A mix of natural materials
- **b.** The finest silk
- **c.** Lamb's wool
- **d.** Cotton from Africa

2. When will Sloan's clothes be available in Japan?
- **a.** March
- **b.** June
- **c.** September
- **d.** December

3. What can you infer about Sloan's from the passage?
- **a.** The clothes are quite cheap.
- **b.** The clothes are fairly expensive.
- **c.** The clothes are for a small number of people.
- **d.** The clothes are meant to be relaxed in.

4. What kinds of clothes are not mentioned in the passage?
- **a.** Beach clothes
- **b.** Clothes for children
- **c.** Casual clothing
- **d.** Office clothing

5. What do you know about Sloan's from the passage?
- **a.** You can buy the clothes before the stores open.
- **b.** The company uses Asian designers.
- **c.** It is a Chinese company.
- **d.** Most of the clothes will be sold on the Internet.

Conversation 2

Track 50 Beth has found the sportswear department and now wants to try on clothes. Listen to the conversation and fill in the missing words.

Beth: I was just looking at your hoodies, and I love this ❶ ________, but I wish you had one in red.

Clerk: Actually, we do. I'll go and get one for you. Um, what size do you take, ❷ ________ or large?

Beth: I'll try a large. I want it to feel nice and comfortable.

Clerk: OK, I'll fetch that for you.

Beth: Before you go, do you have any more ❸ ________ in the store? These ones here are beautiful, but they're quite ❹ ________ and I want something more ❺ ________.

Clerk: There are a few more over there next to the ❻ ________.

Beth: Great, thanks.

Clerk: Here's your hoodie. I see you've ❼ ________ a few tank tops. Do you want to try them on?

Beth: Yes, please. I wish I could buy them all, but I don't have enough money. Anyway, where's the ❽ ________?

Clerk: It's just around the corner. Feel free to call me over if you need any help getting different sizes or colors of any of the ❾ ________.

Beth: I will do, thanks. Oh, the hoodie you've brought me is a medium.

Clerk: I am sorry, that was accidental. I'll bring you the correct size now.

Words to Remember

Use the words in the box to complete the questions and answers below.

item	*fitting*	*sweatshirt*	*loose*	*fitting room*
pick out	*medium*	*tank top*	*design*	

1. **Q:** How does it feel? Is it big enough?
   A: No, it's a little ________.
2. **Q:** Why don't you put a ________ on?
   A: I don't like showing off my arms.
3. **Q:** Where's Jenny?
   A: She in the ________ trying on clothes.
4. **Q:** What kind of magazine would you like?
   A: Anything. Just ________ one for me.
5. **Q:** Do you like the ________ of this T-shirt?
   A: No, I think it's ugly.

Get It Right

A. Read the following passage about one's clothing preferences.

I like to wear casual clothing like jeans, T-shirts, and sweatshirts, and I usually wear sneakers on my feet instead of shoes. I don't like wearing things like dress pants and shirts because they aren't comfortable, and when I put them on, I feel that I can't really relax.

I buy most of clothes from sports stores or sportswear sections outlets in department stores. I often get my jeans from the supermarket because they're a lot cheaper than the ones on sale at jeans stores. I wish I had more money to spend on clothes because I would definitely get myself some nicer things.

I also wish it were possible to dress casually all the time, but when I go to work or to a dinner party, I tend to put on something a lot more formal. I did wear my jeans to work once, but I wished I hadn't as my boss was angry with me.

B. What kinds of clothes do you like to wear, and wear do you normally buy them? If you wear different things for different occasions, you can write about that. Try to use "wish" in your answer.

Grammar Bite

***Wish* can be used to talk about things you want to be true. It can be used in past, present, and future tense sentences.**

1. The past	2. The present	3. The future
• I *wish* I had arrived earlier. • She *wishes* she could have done that yesterday.	• He *wishes* he were stronger. • I *wish* I were playing soccer with my friends.	• I *wish* I could meet you tomorrow. • They *wish* won't have a test tomorrow.

Give It a Try

Use the following sentences to help you write new sentences using *wish*. The first one has been done for you.

1. I slept late last night.
   I wish I had slept earlier last night.
2. I'm not good at basketball.
   ____
3. She doesn't have good grades.
   ____
4. The boys are not going to the party.
   ____
5. Mr. Graham can't watch the movie later.
   ____

Prepare Yourself

Look at the floor plans of a department store below. Where would you want to go if you went shopping here?

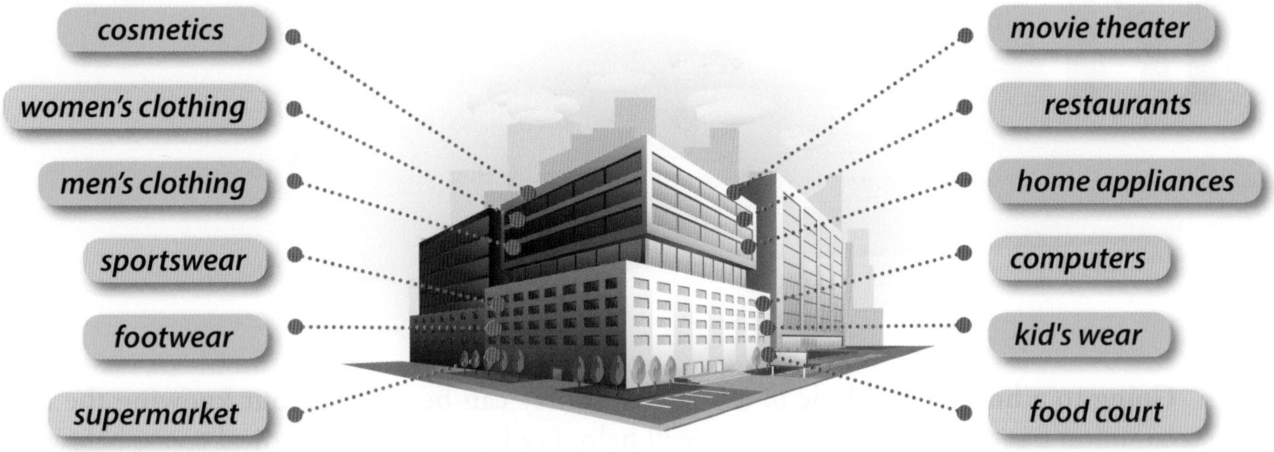

Activity 1

With your partner, take turns asking for directions to different departments.

Activity 2

Imagine that you are choosing clothes in a department store and that your partner is a store clerk. Ask for different items in different colors and sizes.

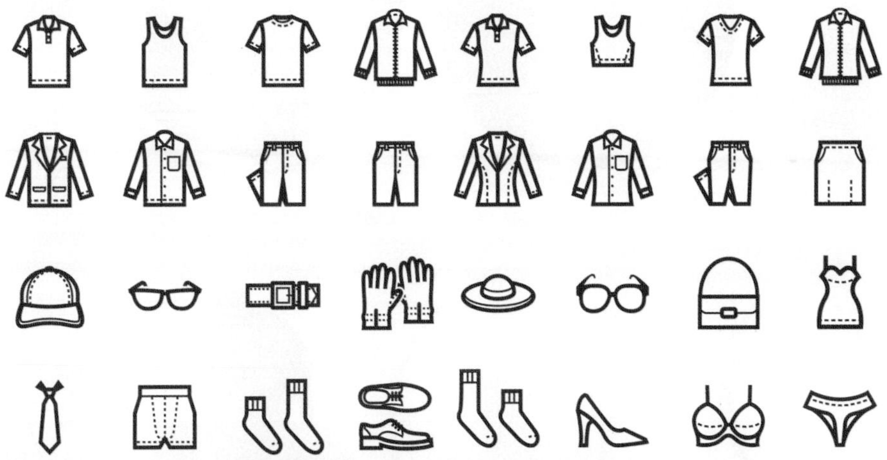

red	blue	yellow	black	purple	pink	green	brown	grey	white

XL – extra large, L – large, M – medium, S – small, XS – extra small

Useful Expressions

- Do you have these pants in *medium*?
- I don't suppose you have *this skirt* in *dark blue*, do you?
- I just want to check whether you have my size – I take an *extra large*.
- Could I get a *small* one of these in *light green*?

Unit 14

Illness and Injury

By the end of this unit, you will be able to do the following:

- Ask for medicine
- Ask for and give medical advice
- Use narrative tenses to tell stories

Before We Go

Going to a hospital or clinic in a foreign country can be difficult, but knowing the names of common treatments and procedures will help. Look at the list of medical terms below, and use them to label the pictures.

band aid	*sling*	*cast*	*painkiller*
stretcher	*bandage*	*X-ray*	*injection*

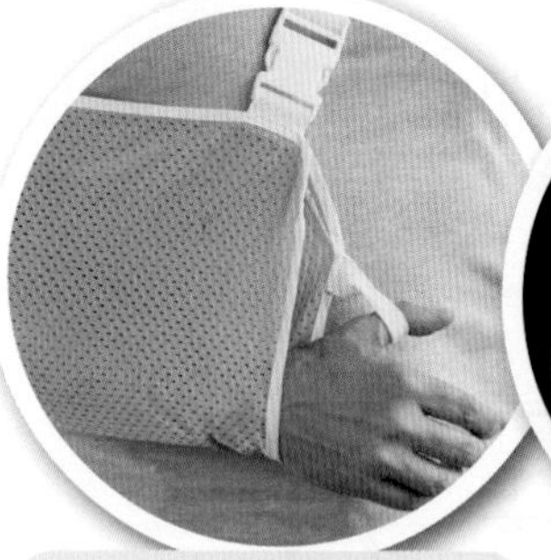

❶

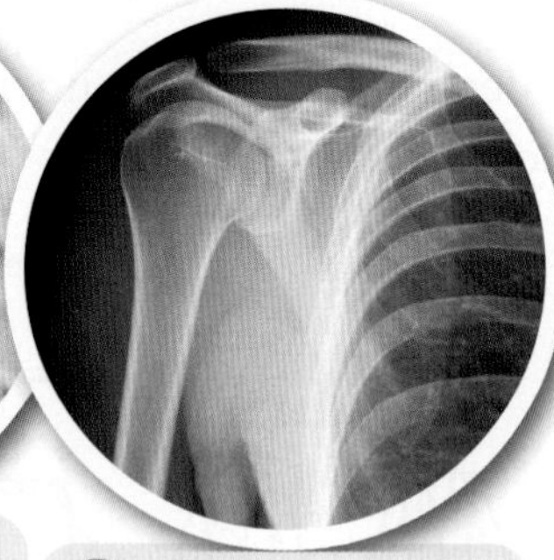

❷

❸

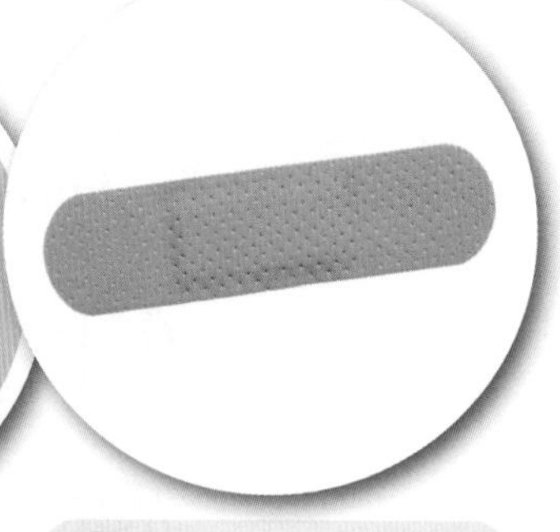

❹

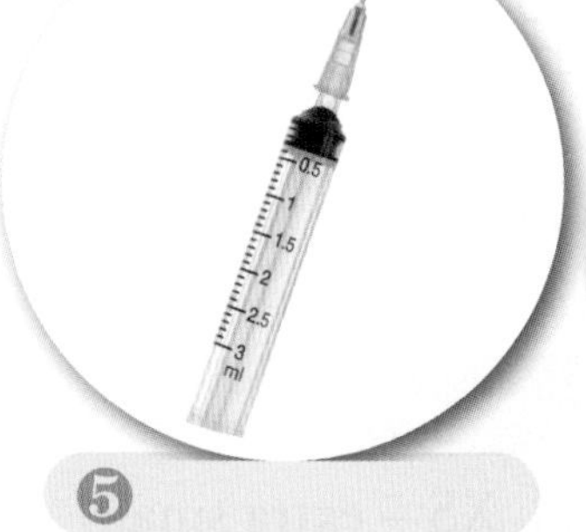

❺

❻

❼

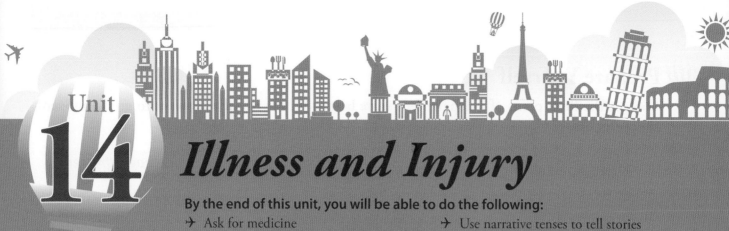

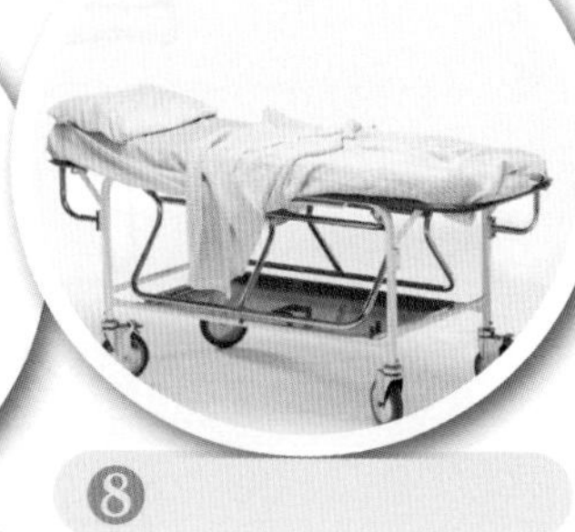

❽

Useful Expressions

- I went to a hospital *once* when *I broke my arm.*
- If I *cut my finger*, I would *put a band aid on it.*
- I once *got a nasty cut on my forehead.*
- I've been to hospital lots of times, *but never for anything serious.*

Conversation 1

Track 51 Martin is suffering with allergies on his vacation, so he goes to a pharmacy for some medicine. Listen to the conversation and fill in the missing words.

Martin: Hi, there. Do you have any good medicine for allergies? I can't seem to stop sneezing.

Pharmacist: We've got a few things you can try. Do you know what could be causing the problem, or could you tell me when the sneezing is at its worst?

Martin: I don't really know; it seems to be pretty much constant.

Pharmacist: OK, well in that case you might want to try using this ❶ ______. It's very strong, and it should work ❷ ______.

Martin: Do you have any ❸ ______? I've always hated using nasal sprays.

Pharmacist: We do. These ones are very effective, but they might cause ❹ ______.

Martin: That's OK; I'll take them before bed. They'll help me sleep.

Pharmacist: I can see that your eyes are quite red, as well. Would you like some ❺ ______? They should reduce feelings of ❻ ______.

Martin: Yes, please. I was going to ask you about them. There's one more thing. As you can probably see, I was out in the sun a bit too long today, and my ❼ ______ is killing me. Do you sell ❽ ______ here?

Pharmacist: Yes, we do. We've got a few different kinds on the shelf next to the door. I think you might need a big bottle!

Martin: Yeah, you're right. I fell asleep on the beach. I'm never going to do that again.

Pharmacist: Right, you should look after yourself.

Martin: I will, thank you

Words to Remember

Use the words in the box to complete the sentences.

pill	*nasal spray*	*allergy*	*itchiness*	*eye drops*
pharmacy	*immediately*	*drowsiness*	*sunburn*	*aloe vera*

1. The students left the classroom ______ after the class finished. They didn't wait at all.
2. Sally went to the ______ to get some medicine for her headache.
3. Because of my ______, I sneeze whenever I'm around cats.
4. Sam has terrible ______. His skin is very red.
5. You shouldn't drive after taking medicine that causes ______.

Reading

Track 52 **Doctors sometimes give patients advice as well as medicine. Read the instructions given to people by their doctors, and look up any words you don't know.**

Patient: Ian Holloway   Doctor: Dr. Grey

I'm not giving you any medicine. What you really need is rest and relaxation. Try and stay in bed all day, and if you do not go out, make sure that you sleep early. In addition, drink lots of water, as this will help your body recover more quickly. Vitamin C will also be good for you. You can take tablets, but it would be better if you had fruit – oranges are very good.

Patient: Sandy Regan   Doctor: Dr. Shepherd

I've applied cream to your wound and put a bandage over it. Every day before you go to bed, take off the bandage, put on some cream, and cover it with a new bandage. It's very important that you keep the wound and bandage dry. If it does get wet, dry it quickly with clean paper towels, apply cream, and put on a new, dry bandage. Your hand should be OK in about five days. If the wound gets worse or starts to feel very itchy, come back to see me.

Give It a Try

Read the advice again and choose the best response to each of the following questions.

1. What is likely to be wrong with Ian Holloway?
   a. Heart problems **b.** A cold **c.** A broken bone **d.** A burn
2. When will Sandy Regan be able to stop wearing a bandage?
   a. A couple of days **b.** Almost a week **c.** A week **d.** Over a week
3. Why wasn't Ian Holloway given any medicine?
   a. He doesn't need it. **b.** It would make her recover slower. **c.** She needs to rest first. **d.** It would stop him sleeping.
4. Where could Ian Holloway get vitamin C?
   a. Milkshake **b.** Ice cream **c.** Medicine **d.** Fruit juice
5. What doesn't Sandy Regan need to look after her wound?
   a. Pills **b.** An injection **c.** A bandage **d.** Water

Conversation 2

Track 53 After Martin had an accident on his rented scooter and hurt his hand, he went to the hospital emergency room. Listen to the conversation and fill in the missing words.

Martin: I fell off my scooter earlier today and hurt my hand. You can see that there's a deep cut here, and my ❶ ______ is really hurting.

Doctor: OK, well I think we should sort out the cut first. I think it will take four stitches to close up this cut, but I'll get the nurse to clean out the wound first. It looks like you've got some ❷ ______ in it. How did this happen?

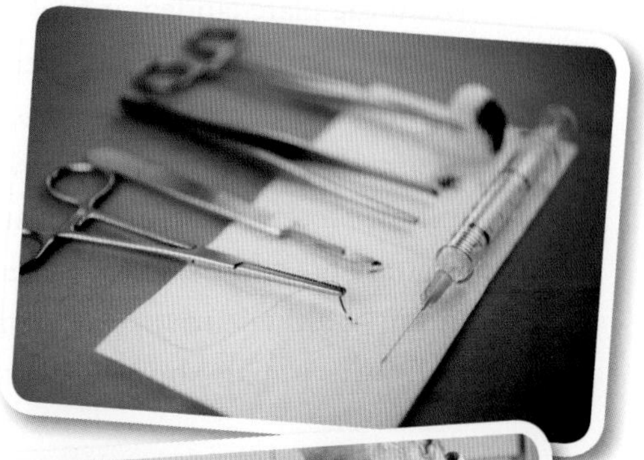

Martin: I have been in the city for a few days, but I hadn't seen the surrounding area so I rented a scooter. When I was riding past the train station, though I was ❸ ______ by a car.

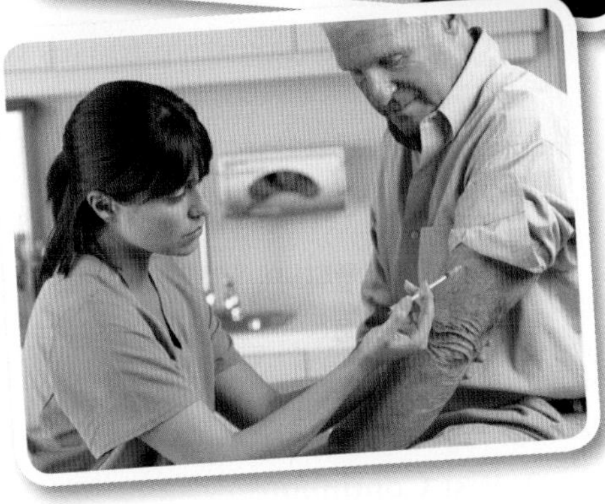

Doctor: That doesn't sound good.

Martin: No, as soon as I hit the ❹ ______, I knew something was wrong. But ❺ ______ the man who hit me drove me to the hospital. Do you think my ring finger is broken?

Doctor: There's a good possibility of that, but I'll need to get you an X-ray to make sure. Right now, though, I'm going to give you an anesthetic so you won't feel anything when we put in the stitches.

Martin: OK.

Doctor: The ❻ ______ will still hurt, but after that, I'll be as quick as ❼ ______ with the stitches.

Martin: Don't worry. I'm as strong as an ❽ ______.

Words to Remember

Use the words in the box to complete the passage below.

ox	*bump*	*lightning*	*emergency room*
grit	*tarmac*	*at least*	*ring finger*

One stormy night last week, Farmer Smith was taking his ❶ ______ into his barn when ❷ ______ struck the building. Some bricks fell on the farmer's head, leaving him with a terrible ❸ ______. His wife drove him to the ❹ ______, but when he got there, he had to wait ❺ ______ an hour before a doctor saw him. It wasn't a serious injury, though, and he was soon able to go home with his wife.

Get It Right

A. Read the following short article about one's experience visiting the hospital.

When I was ten years old, I was taken to hospital after I cut my wrist. I got the injury after I slipped at home. I had been carrying a plate of food, and when the plate landed, it broke and one of the pieces left a deep cut on my arm. My dad said that I needed stitches and drove me to the emergency room. I had never had a serious injury before, so I felt a bit scared. The hospital was busy when we arrived there, and I was waiting about 30 minutes to see a doctor. Eventually, a friendly doctor came to look at my wound and told me I would need one stitch. Before she put it in, she gave me an anesthetic to take away the pain. My hospital experience was not very bad. I was in pain, but the doctors and nurses were all very nice.

B. Now, use narrative tenses to write a short story about a visit you have made to the hospital.

Grammar Bite

Narrative tenses are verb tenses that are used to tell stories about things in the past. There are four tenses that you can use to tell the story.

1. **Past Simple**
   - I *went* to the gym at 1 p.m.
   - Janice *ate* her dinner at a French restaurant.
2. **Past Continuous**
   - Amy was *cooking* dinner last night.
   - Bruce *was watching* TV this afternoon.
3. **Past Perfect**
   - He *had taken* the bus to school for years.
   - Jerry *had listened* to this radio program for several hours.
4. **Past Perfect Continuous**
   - They *had been having* trouble with their car for weeks.
   - Aaron *had been practicing* his Spanish for a month.

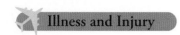

Give It a Try

Use narrative tenses to make sentences from the following words and phrases.

1. Tom / eat / I came home (Past Continuous)

   ____

2. She / sleep / well / last night (Past Simple)

   ____

3. The boys / fight / 10 minutes (Past Perfect Continuous)

   ____

4. My mom / finish / the cake / already (Past Perfect)

   ____

5. I / write / the report / my computer (Past Simple)

   ____

Prepare Yourself

Look at the pictures below. They all show people suffering medical problems, but what's wrong with each of them?

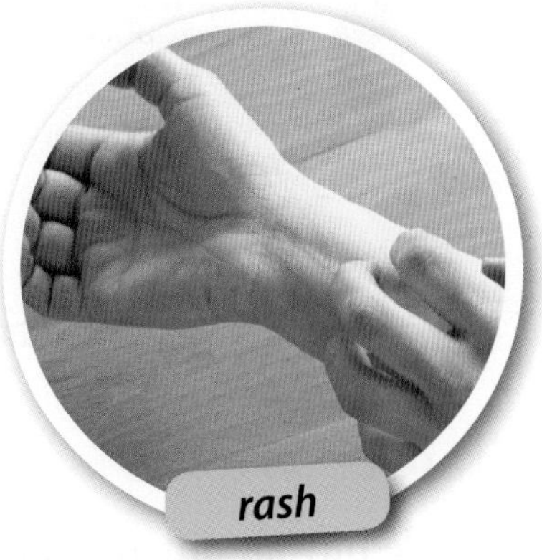

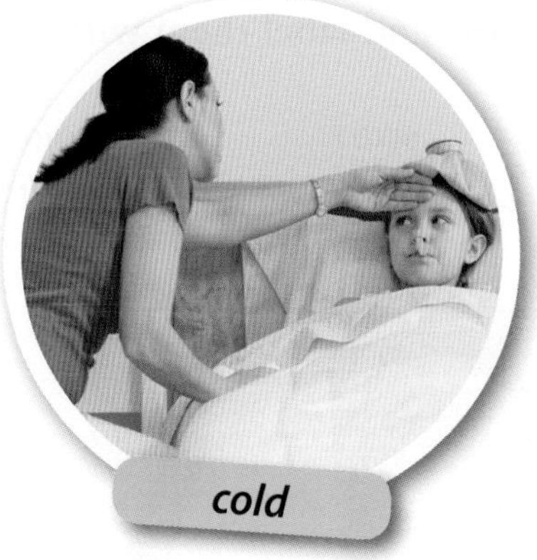

Activity 1

With your partner, take turns saying that you have one of these problems and asking for advice.

Activity 2

Read what happened to these people and talk to your partner about what you think they should do.

Todd

Todd was ironing his clothes and accidentally put the hot iron down on his hand.

Emma

Emma was walking to the store when she fell and scratched her knee.

Rose

Rose fell from her horse and landed on her ankle. She is now having trouble standing up.

Useful Expressions

- I have a terrible *cold*. What do you think I should do?
- It's not a big problem. Just *try to take it easy*.
- Get some rest and see what happens. If it *gets worse, go and see a doctor*.
- If I were you, I would go to *a pharmacy to get some medicine*.

Unit 15

Buying Souvenirs

By the end of this unit, you will be able to do the following:

- Bargain for souvenirs
- Use compound words
- Make suggestions
- Write about past experiences

Before We Go

People buy all different kinds of things to remind them of their vacations. Take a look at the souvenirs below and label them with the words from the box.

postcard	*scarf*	*bookmark*	*carving*
key ring	*bracelet*	*handicraft*	*snow globe*

❶ ____ ❷ ____ ❸ ____ ❹ ____

❺ ____ ❻ ____ ❼ ____ ❽ ____

Useful Expressions

- I love buying *snow globes* on vacations. I collect them.
- I keep vacation souvenirs on my *bookshelf*.
- I never spend much money on *souvenirs*.

Conversation 1

Track 54 Grace is walking through a tourist market when she sees some wooden chess sets.

Vendor: I can see you're interested in the chess sets. They make great souvenirs.

Grace: I'm sure they do. What kind of wood is this? It's really pretty.

Vendor: It's ❶ ______. It comes from the forests just outside the city. Would you like to buy one? I can give you a good ❷ ______.

Grace: How much are you asking for this one?

Vendor: I can sell that one to you for $100.

Grace: You can't be serious! I won't pay that much. I'll give you $10 for it.

Vendor: What? This set is ❸ ______ a lot more than that. The wood is very ❹ ______, and it was hand made by ❺ ______ ❻ ______.

Grace: Maybe, but $100 is way too much. If you want me to buy it, you need to bring the price down.

Vendor: OK, OK, you seem like a nice lady, so just for you, I'm prepared to sell the set for $70.

Grace: That's still too much. How does $25 sound?

Vendor: ❼ ______.

Grace: Alright, maybe I'll try and find a nice chess set somewhere else. Bye.

Vendor: OK, wait, wait. $55, but that's the ❽ ______ price.

Grace: Hmm…$35, and that's as high as I can go.

Vendor: $45.

Grace: ❾ ______.

Words to Remember

Use the words in the box to complete the questions and answers.

deal	*terrible*	*valuable*	*done*	*rock bottom*
worth	*chess*	*craftsman*	*local*	*sandalwood*

1. **Q:** If you help me with my homework, I'll give you my cake. OK? **A:** ______.
2. **Q:** Do you live in the ______ area?
   A: No, I live in another city.
3. **Q:** How much do you think this car is ______?
   A: Not much; it's really old.
4. **Q:** What did the tutor say about your homework?
   A: She said it was ______.
5. **Q:** How are you feeling today? You look worse than yesterday.
   A: I feel awful. I think I'm at ______.

Reading

Track 55 **Bargaining for souvenirs is a common practice in many tourist destinations around the world. It can sometimes be difficult to get a good price, but by following the advice below, you should be able to get what you want without spending too much.**

Bargaining, or haggling, for souvenirs is not easy, and you might need to spend some time negotiating if you don't want to pay too much.

Before you ask how much something is, have an idea in your head about how much it's worth to you. Once you're sure of this, don't be affected by the figure the vendor gives you as they may say a figure many times higher than the object's actual worth.

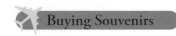

When you reply, feel free to make an offer that's much lower than what you want to pay. This will give you room to negotiate later. Remain calm and friendly while you haggle. If the vendor genuinely likes you, you'll find it easier to get a good deal.

If the vendor is reluctant to bring the price down, you could pretend to give up and walk away. If you're being asked to pay too much, you're likely to be called back and offered a lower price.

It's also a good idea to ask about several items. If you show too much interest in one thing, you're likely to be asked to pay more for it.

Finally, don't take haggling too seriously. Often, tourists end up arguing about amounts of money that aren't important to them, but it might still mean a lot to the vendor.

Give It a Try

Read the advice again and choose the best responses to each of the following questions.

1. What should you do if you're given a very high price?
   - **a.** Get angry.
   - **b.** Look confused.
   - **c.** Act surprised.
   - **d.** Walk away.
2. Why should you be friendly when you haggle?
   - **a.** It might help you pay less.
   - **b.** You might get extra things.
   - **c.** You'll enjoy the experience more.
   - **d.** You could make friends.
3. What should you do before you ask about prices?
   - **a.** Look around many stores.
   - **b.** Count your money.
   - **c.** Be sure what you want to buy.
   - **d.** Decide how much to pay.
4. How would you give yourself room to negotiate?
   - **a.** Remain calm.
   - **b.** Set a low price.
   - **c.** Don't be affected by the vendor.
   - **d.** Say how much you want to pay.
5. What advice is given in the passage?
   - **a.** Don't haggle too slowly.
   - **b.** Try to buy more than one thing.
   - **c.** Don't get angry.
   - **d.** Focus on what you want to buy.

Conversation 2

Track 56 **Grace and her husband, Peter, talk about the gifts they can buy for their relatives.**

Grace: So we've bought a pen for your mother and a carving for your father. Now we need something for my parents.

Peter: I never know what to get for them. We could just buy some cookies or dried fruit.

Grace: No. They said they didn't want snacks. They told me they were both going on ❶ ______.

Peter: Alright then, why not get some of those ❷ ______ ❸ ______ — you know, the ones that are made by traditional artists. We saw some beautiful ones yesterday near the hotel.

Grace: I don't think they'd like that kind of stuff. Besides, those cloths are really expensive.

Peter: Then I'm all out of ideas. You suggest something.

Grace: Well, for my dad, I think we could get a nice ❹ ______ — you know how much he likes to read. I've seen some really nice ❺ ______ metal ones.

Peter: Great, and what about your mom? If we can't think of anything else, we could get her another scarf.

Grace: No, we can't. She told me last month that she had already got more scarves than she could ever wear. Why don't we give her some soap?

Peter: Soap? Really? You can buy that anywhere.

Grace: I'm talking about special soap. Don't you remember seeing some in the gift store last week? The saleslady said it was ❻ ______ with local flowers and ❼ ______. It looked nice as well.

Peter: OK, then. Let's go do some shopping.

Words to Remember

Use the words in the box to complete the sentences below.

diet	*engrave*	*ingredient*	*scent*
cloth	*weave*	*relative*	*bookmark*

1. Instead of going on a ______ to lose weight. I'm going to do more exercise.
2. I forgot to use my ______, and now I don't know what page I'm on.
3. The cake was ______ with vanilla.
4. What ______ do you need to make dinner tonight?
5. The trophy was ______ with the name of the winning team.

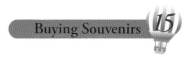

Get It Right

A. Read the passage below. Find out how to write about your experience buying souvenirs.

I've been on many vacations, and I would always buy myself souvenirs. I would usually buy something small, but when I was in Kenya a few years ago, I bought myself a large wooden face mask. While I was in the coastal city of Mombasa, I would often wander through a tourist market. I spotted the face mask one day and knew it would look good on my wall. My friends would buy paintings or carvings of elephants, but all I wanted was the mask. The vendor saw what I was looking at and told me he could give me a good price. The figure he gave me was very high, though, so I said he needed to bring the price down. We haggled for about five minutes before we came to an agreement. He told me I was buying the mask cheaply, but I knew he wasn't telling me the truth. I didn't care. He was a nice guy, and he probably needed the extra money more than I did.

B. Now, write about a vacation you have had and the experience you had buying souvenirs. What did you buy? Did you haggle over the price? What did you and the salesperson say to each other? Try to use *would* in your passage.

Grammar Bite

***Would* is often used to introduce things that regularly happened in the past. The word is generally followed by an adverb of time, for example:**

- He *would* often go the movies.
- She *would* never eat that much again.

1. *Would* is used in statements.
   - I *would* usually have sandwiches for lunch at school.
   - He *would* play soccer every day.
2. *Would* can also be used in questions.
   - *Would* you study hard in elementary school?
   - What *would* you do on the weekend when you were younger?

Give It a Try

Answer the following questions using *would*.

1. Where did you eat when you were younger?

   ____

2. What did you use to do in your free time?

   ____

3. When did you usually go to bed at university?

   ____

4. How did you go to school?

   ____

5. Who did you normally talk to if you felt bad?

   ____

Prepare Yourself

What kind of souvenirs would you expect to buy in the locations shown below?

Activity 1

With your partner, talk about what you would get yourself as a souvenir if you went on vacation to these places? Then choose two other people – your parents, brother, sister, friends – and say what you would get for them as well.

Activity 2

Practice your bargaining skills with a partner. One of you should be a tourist and one of you should be a vendor. You should both negotiate to get the best deal possible.

Useful Expressions

- I would get myself a *model of a London black taxi* because *they're a great symbol of the city.*
- I would get myself a *scarf* from Bangkok because *I know they're cheap and always look good.*
- My father loves *snow globes*, so I would get him one of those.
- My friend collects key rings, and I know *she would love one from New York.*

Units 13-15 REVIEW 5

Listening

A. Track 57 Listen to the speakers and choose the best responses.

1. **a.** If I were you, I would take some painkillers first.
   b. I think you can go and buy some sunblock.
   c. Try putting on some aloe vera. It should help.
   d. You should probably go see a doctor about it.
2. **a.** She loves jewelry, so I will get her a bracelet.
   b. My mom generally keeps souvenirs in a closet.
   c. I promised her I won't spend too much on souvenirs.
   d. Well, I'm not sure if she collects vacation souvenirs.
3. **a.** I don't think the large would suit you.
   b. No, the large one is probably better.
   c. You'll have to wait for that jacket.
   d. Yes, what color would you like?

B. Track 58 Listen to the conversation and choose the best answer to each question.

1. What does the woman mean?
   a. She thinks the painkillers will work very well.
   b. She wants the man to go to the hospital with her.
   c. She feels scared about having to go see a doctor.
   d. She is happy that the man can give her stitches.
2. What kind of injury might the woman have?
   a. A cut from using a knife
   b. An allergy from eating nuts
   c. Sunburn from lying in the sun
   d. A cold from having a cold shower

C. Track 59 Listen to the short talk. Then, circle *True* or *False* for each sentence.

1. The speaker is talking about a new branch of a department store. True / False
2. This place is aimed only at people who are interested in fashion. True / False
3. You can find a selection of designer boutiques here. True / False

Vocabulary

Choose the correct answer for each sentence.

1. Remember to hold on to the hand rail when you're on the _____.
   a. ground floor **b.** escalator **c.** elevator **d.** food court

2. I love this scent. Is it ______?
   a. handicraft b. valuable c. sandalwood d. woven
3. It's normal to experience some ______ after taking this medicine. Don't worry.
   a. stitches b. sunburn c. emergency d. drowsiness
4. That's a terrible ______. I'm sure we can find something cheaper.
   a. ingredient b. deal c. carving d. worth
5. I love the ______ of this skirt. Too bad it only comes in small and medium.
   a. fitting b. fashion c. promotion d. design

Reading Comprehension

Read the following passage and choose the best answer to each question.

Buying souvenirs can be trickier than it sounds. Whether you're buying for yourself or someone else, you'll want to come home with something that's valuable, not something that's going to end up in the junk drawer. To make your next vacation and souvenir-shopping experience a little easier, here are a few helpful tips on souvenir buying.

Pick a meaningful souvenir. We want something that will remind us of our trip. With that in mind, it should be easy to steer clear of T-shirts and sweatshirts; you can get them anywhere. A better choice might be a cookbook filled with regional recipes, or a beautiful shell you found on the beach that you're visiting (not every souvenir needs to be bought).

Pictures can be the best mementos. Instead of buying a lot of random souvenirs to fill your suitcases, choose just one: a themed photo album that reminds you of the place that you're visiting. When you get home, fill it with all the photos from the trip.

How to get your souvenirs home. Your best bet would be to simply not buy too many souvenirs, but this can be easier said than done. One way to accomplish this is to try to wait till the end of your stay before buying anything. Spend your time window shopping, and before you leave, buy the few things that you just have to have.

With careful planning, you can end up with souvenirs that you really like, and get them home without hassle.

1. According to the author, what is NOT true about souvenirs?
   a. They have to be expensive. c. They should be bought early.
   b. They have to be memorable. d. They have to mean something to you.
2. What does "steer clear of" probably mean?
   a. To find b. To help c. To avoid d. To choose
3. What is the main theme of this passage?
   a. How to find the best souvenir. c. How to make sure the souvenirs are memorable.
   b. How to get the right things for the right people. d. How to buy souvenirs you won't regret buying.

Unit 1 Trip of a Lifetime

There are many different kinds of vacations you can go on to see the world. Look at the following pictures of different trips. Use the vacation terms in the box to label each picture.

adventure trip	*bicycle tour*	*cruise*	*cultural tour*
ecotourism	*food tour*	*luxury trip*	*volunteer vacation*

❶ ______

❷ ______

❸ ______

❹ ______

❺ ______

❻ ______

❼ ______

❽ ______

Useful Expressions

- I would most like to go on *a cruise* because *I enjoy the service.*
- I don't think that I would ever want to try *bicycle trip.*
- That kind of trip allows you to *have fun, help others, and make friends.*
- I know someone who went on *a safari.* He/She thought it was *exciting.*
- I like See Europe in STYLE because it offers *a theater trip.*
- I think Hawaii Life Tours would be the best trip because it offers *luxury vacations.*
- I would recommend that trip to *Mark* because he likes *cities,* and he can visit them on that trip.

Unit 2 How Much Should I Bring?

Depending on where you go on vacation, deciding what to take with you can be either difficult or almost impossible. Look at the picture of vacation essentials below, and use the words from the box to correctly label each item.

sun cream	*guide book*	*swimsuit*	*sunglasses*
toiletry bag	*passport*	*foreign currency*	*credit card*

1 ____________ 2 ____________ 3 ____________ 4 ____________

5 ____________ 6 ____________ 7 ____________ 8 ____________

Useful Expressions

- I always pack a *guide book* when I go on vacation because *they're very helpful*.
- I rarely take a *credit card*; I don't think they're important.
- I think *toiletry bags* are essential because *you always want to be clean and fresh*.
- The first thing I think of when packing is my *passport*.
- For money, I will *take traveler's checks* and *cash*.
- I will pack *a swimsuit* because I will be *going to the beach*.
- I'll probably want my *book* on the flight, so I will put it in my hand luggage.
- I will put my *camera* in my luggage since I won't need it until I arrive.

Unit 3 Meeting Other Travelers

When you go on vacation, especially if you join a tour group, you'll meet a lot of new people with different characteristics. Look at the pictures of people below and use the list of characteristics from the box to describe what each person is like.

outgoing	*shy*	*thoughtful*	*funny*
serious	*childish*	*gloomy*	*arrogant*

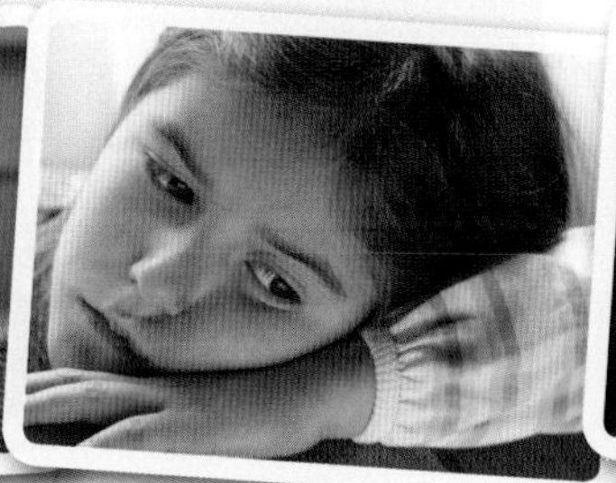

1 ____________ 2 ____________ 3 ____________ 4 ____________

5

6

7

8

Useful Expressions

- You'll *love* him; he's always so *funny*
- She can be a little *childish*, but she is *nice*.
- He's usually *shy* when he *first meets people*, but that changes when he *gets to know them*.
- I'm a fairly *thoughtful* person.
- One of my biggest interests is *sport*. I love *tennis*.
- I think I'd like *Mike* the most. We seem to have a lot in common.
- I'd get along well with *Rachel*. She seems really interesting.

Unit 4 Checking In / Out

When you check in and out of a hotel, you'll almost certainly find the check-in desk in the hotel lobby. Look at the list of things you'll see in a lobby and use the terms to label the pictures.

check-in desk	*concierge*	*luggage cart*	*bar*
escalator	*bellhop*	*information desk*	*elevator*

1

2

3

4

5

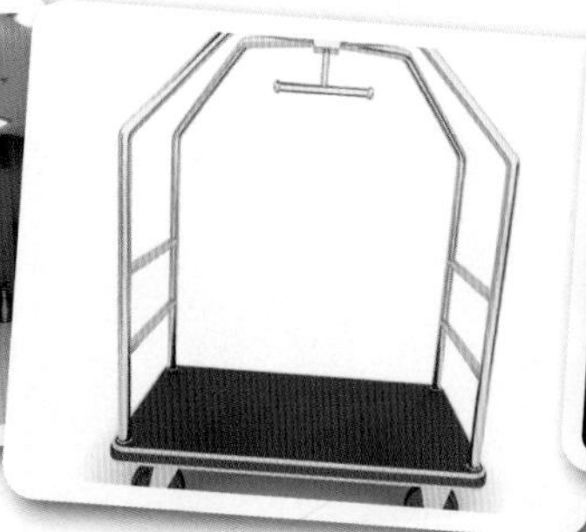

6

7

8

Useful Expressions

- I have a room reserved under the name *Amy Roberts*.
- I'd like to check in, please. I booked *a double room*; it's in the name of *Singh*.
- I'd like to check out of *Room 213*.
- What time will *breakfast* be served?
- What time does the *pool close in the evening*?
- I need to get to the *airport*. Can you tell me the quickest way to get there?
- How much would a taxi to *the train station* cost?

Unit 5 Room Service

In many hotels, you can order room service and have food brought to your room, but this usually isn't the only in-room service available. Take a look at the list of services below and use the terms to label the picture.

massage	*housekeeping*	*unpacking service*	*laundry*
in-room movie	*room service*	*luxury bath*	*Internet connection*

❶

❷

❸

❹

❺

❻

❼

❽

Useful Expressions

- I would love to have a *luxury bath*.
- I'm not interested in the *laundry service* because I *always pack enough clothes*.
- The *unpacking service* looks interesting. I might ask about that on my next vacation.
- I often use the *in-room movie* service in hotels.
- I think it would be great to try the *luxury bath service* because *it would help me relax*.
- The most useful service would be the *Wi-Fi connection* because *many people take computers with them on vacation now*.
- I'd like to order *chicken nuggets* and *fried rice* please.
- Does the *apple pie* come with *ice cream*?

Unit 6 Hotel Facilities

In addition to in-room services, hotels provide a range of other services to keep their guests happy and com fortable. There are rooms and areas set aside for entertainment, business, sports and relaxation. Look at the list of services below, and use the terms to label the pictures.

gym	*business center*	*games area*	*restaurant*
sauna	*children's play area*	*lounge bar*	*hair and nails salon*

① ② ③ ④

⑤ ⑥ ⑦ ⑧

Useful Expressions

- Some hotels charge you for using the *business center*, but others don't.
- I've never used a *hotel spa*, so I don't know if they're free.
- *Gyms* are always free.
- *Hair and nails salons* can be quite expensive.
- We should tell people not to *eat* in the *gym* because *it will get the room dirty*.
- There should be *a limit* on how long people can use the computers in the business center.
- I don't think *lounge bars* need rules; everybody knows what they're supposed to do there.
- *Paul* should *ask whether the machine can be fixed. He might have to go to the front desk.*
- If I were him, I would probably *just ignore the problem and use a different machine.*

Unit 7 All About Breakfast

Many hotels provide large, all-you-can-eat breakfasts with a range of hot and cold dishes from many different countries placed around the dining room. Have a look at the list of foods below and use the names to label the foods.

cereal	*pancake*	*sausage*	*baked beans*
bacon	*croissant*	*scrambled eggs*	*hash brown*

❶

❷

❸

❹

❺

❻

❼

❽

Useful Expressions

- I like to eat *sausages, fried eggs,* and *hash browns*, but I know they're *unhealthy*.
- I usually start my day with *cereal* because *it tastes good and gives me energy*.
- I love *croissants*, and I don't often get to have *them* at home.
- I would offer *croissants* because I think they're delicious.
- I've chosen *cereal* because *millions of people eat it every morning*.
- I wouldn't have *waffles* because *I don't think they're breakfast foods*.

Unit 8 Making a Reservation

Before making a reservation, you have to decide on what kind of restaurant you want to go to. Have a look at the list of restaurant types below and use the terms to label the pictures.

sushi bar	*French bistro*	*Indian restaurant*	*American diner*
pizzeria	*hot pot restaurant*	*vegetarian restaurant*	*seafood restaurant*

❶

❷

❸

❹

5

6

7

8

Useful Expressions

- I love *sushi bars*; the food is so *fresh and tasty*.
- I like going to *American diners* because *the atmosphere is usually very relaxed*.
- I'm not keen on *teppanyaki restaurants* because *I always come out smelling of food*.
- I'm a big fan of *curry*, so I go to *Indian restaurants* as often as I can.
- I like the look of *Pho*. I really enjoy *Vietnamese food*.
- I have a problem with *spicy food*, so I wouldn't want to go to *Curry Heaven*.
- How do you feel about *Veggie Love*? The *"exciting vegetarian menu" looks interesting*.
- I don't have much money, so I'd prefer somewhere less expensive like *Canton Delight*.
- A: Hello, this is *Brushstrokes*. How can I help you?
  B: I'd like to book / reserve a table for *three*.

Unit 9 Dining Etiquette

Does the sight of a fully set table in a high-class restaurant make you nervous? You're not alone. Try to match each word from the box with the appropriate item on the table to better understand the use of each plate, glass, and utensil.

wine glass	*dinner fork*	*salad fork*	*water glass*	*salad plate*
soup spoon	*dinner plate*	*dinner knife*	*napkin*	*table mat*

1 ________

2 ________

3 ________

4 ________

5 ________

6 ________

7 ________

8 ________

9 ________

10 ________

Useful Expressions

- In some countries, it's customary to *tip* waiters *10%*.
- I like fast-food restaurants because *they're fast and informal.*
- I think it's rude to *wear a hat in a restaurant.*
- It's polite to give a gift when *you're invited to someone's house.*
- When visiting a person's home, you should *remain standing until you're invited to sit down.*
- It's very impolite to *take your shoes off in a restaurant.*
- When you're at work, you mustn't *chat on the phone with friends.*
- In my country, you *should shake hands* when meeting someone.

Unit 10

Getting on a Train

Train stations can be busy and confusing places. To help yourself find your way around one, take a look at the pictures and list of vocabulary below. Use the terms to label the pictures.

platform	***ticket barrier***	***information***	***ticket counter***
conductor	***tracks***	***timetable***	***train carriage***

1 ____________ 2 ____________ 3 ____________ 4 ____________

5 ____________ 6 ____________ 7 ____________ 8 ____________

Useful Expressions

- I prefer traveling by *train* to traveling by *bus* because *you can't get stuck in traffic jams.*
- The worst train ride I've ever had was in *Macedonia* when *a policeman pointed a gun at me and asked for my passport.*
- I usually *read* when I'm on the train.
- My best train experience came in France as *the train was so fast and clean.*
- Can you tell me where I can find *the first-class area*?
- It's at the *back* of the train in *carriage nine.*
- There are a few *toilets* on the train. There's one *toilet* area at the *end of each carriage.*
- *Carriage five* is right in the middle of the train.

Unit 11 Car Rentals

Before you rent a car, you have to decide what kind of vehicle you want to drive. Take a look at the pictures of different cars below and use the terms from the box to label them.

sedan	*hatchback*	*convertible*	*automatic*
coupe	*SUV*	*minivan*	*stick shift*

❶ ______

❷ ______

❸ ______

❹ ______

❺ ______

❻ ______

❼ ______

❽ ______

Useful Expressions

- I usually drive *automatic* cars because *they're not as difficult to control*.
- If you're with a lot of people, a *minivan* might be useful.
- If I rent a car on my next vacation I'll get a *convertible* so *I can put down the roof and feel the wind in my hair*.
- I think we all need to *do more to look after the environment*, so I want to drive a hybrid.
- I would advise *Kevin* to get a *minivan* because *they have the most room*?
- I disagree. I think *Kevin* would be better off in *a standard-size sedan* because *he doesn't have much money*.
- Winnie doesn't need *a big car*, so I would rent a *compact* if I were *her*.

Unit 12 Taking a Cruise

Modern cruise ships are huge with many different rooms, decks, and items. Take a look at the terms below and try to match them to the pictures.

bow	*port*	*deck*	*galley*	*cabin*
stern	*starboard*	*bridge*	*gangplank*	*lifeboat*

1 ______

2 ______

3 ______

4 ______

5 ______

6 ______

7 ______

8 ______

9 ______

10 ______

Useful Expressions

- I have never taken a cruise; *they seem to be very expensive.*
- I went on a cruise *once* and *had a great time.*
- I would love to go on a cruise because *it's a great way to relax and see lots of different places.*
- I'm not interested in taking a cruise because *I think I would get bored.*
- I'm more interested in *Royal Oriental cruises* because *I want luxury and a high-class vacation.*
- I think *Playtime Cruises* might be fun, but *there might be too much noise and excitement.*
- I think *older* people would be interested in *Royal Oriental.*
- My guess is that *young families* would get more enjoyment from *Playtime Cruises.*

Unit 13 In a Department Store

Department stores are usually large places with many different floors and sections. Look at the list of departments written below and use them to label the pictures.

food court	*cosmetics*	*home appliances*	*designer boutique*
jewelry	*sportswear*	*home furnishing*	*formal wear*

1 ______

2 ______

3 ______

4 ______

5

6

7

8

Useful Expressions

- I don't go to *department stores* very often. I think they're *too expensive*.
- The first place I usually go in a department store is the *sportswear* department.
- I usually buy *casual* clothing.
- I spend most money in the *home furnishings* department.The exhibition on *medieval Japan* should be interesting. I'm intrigued by *Japanese culture*.
- Do you have these pants in *medium*?
- I don't suppose you have *this skirt* in *dark blue*, do you?
- I just want to check whether you have my size – I take an *extra large*.
- Could I get a *small* one of these in *light green*?

Unit 14 Illness and Injury

Going to a hospital or clinic in a foreign country can be difficult, but knowing the names of common treatments and procedures will help. Look at the list of medical terms below, and use them to label the pictures.

band aid	*sling*	*cast*	*painkiller*
stretcher	*bandage*	*X-ray*	*injection*

1

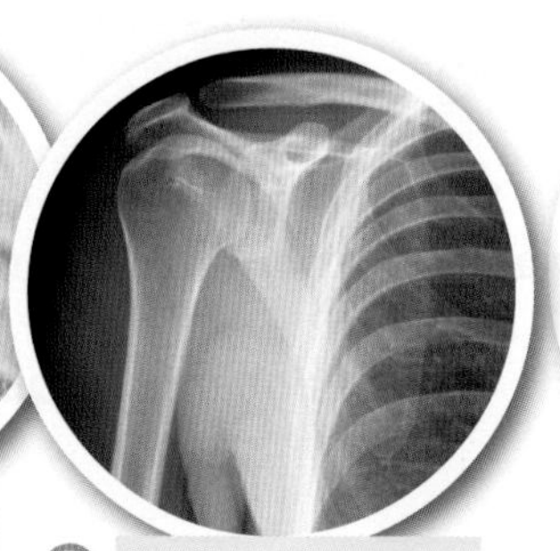

2

3

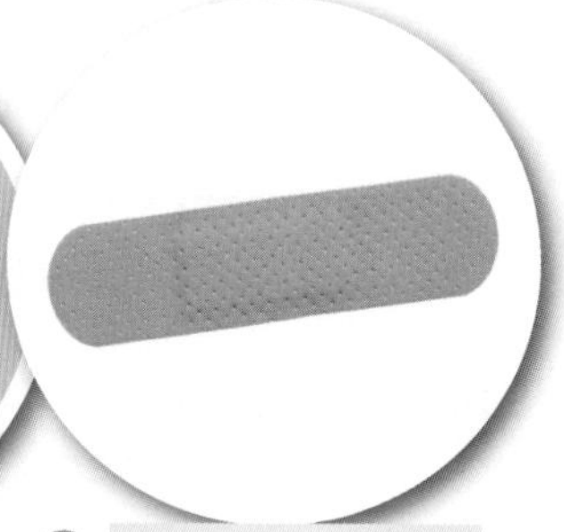

4

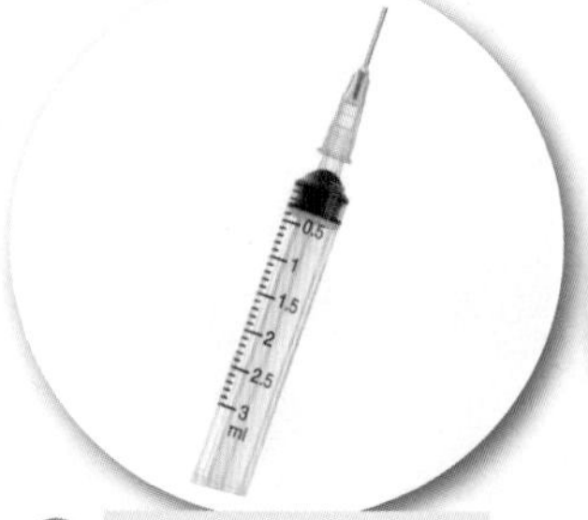

6

7

8

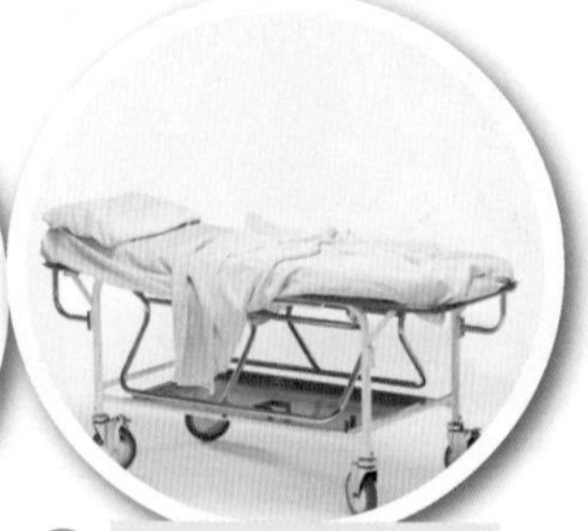

9

Useful Expressions

- I went to a hospital *once* when *I broke my arm.*
- If I *cut my finger,* I would *put a band aid on it.*
- I once *got a nasty cut on my forehead.*
- I've been to hospital lots of times, *but never for anything serious.*
- I have a terrible *cold.* What do you think I should do?
- It's not a big problem. Just *try to take it easy.*
- Get some rest and see what happens. If it *gets worse, go and see a doctor.*
- If I were you, I would go to *a pharmacy to get some medicine.*

Unit 15 Buying Souvenirs

People buy all different kinds of things to remind them of their vacations. Take a look at the souvenirs below and label them with the words from the box.

postcard	*scarf*	*bookmark*	*carving*
key ring	*bracelet*	*handicraft*	*snow globe*

1

2

3

4

5

6

7

8

Useful Expressions

- I love buying *snow globes* on vacations. I collect them.
- I keep vacation souvenirs on my *bookshelf.*
- I never spend much money on *souvenirs.*
- I would get myself a *model of a London black taxi* because *they're a great symbol of the city.*
- I would get myself a *scarf* from Bangkok because *I know they're cheap and always look good.*
- My father loves *snow globes,* so I would get him one of those.
- My friend collects key rings, and I know *she would love one from New York.*

Photo credits

Cover Photos: iStockphoto/Thinkstock

Page 8: (1) Fuse/Thinkstock, (2, 6, 7) iStockphoto/Thinkstock, (3) Wavebreak Media/Thinkstock, (4) Monkey Business/Thinkstock, (5) Lifesize/Thinkstock, (8) Top Photo Group/Thinkstock; **9**: (t) Fuse/Thinkstock, (b) iStockphoto/Thinkstock; **10**: Image Source/ Thinkstock; **11**: (t) Digital Vision/Thinkstock, (b) iStockphoto/Thinkstock; **12-13**: iStockphoto/Thinkstock; **14**: (1, 2, 4-7) iStockphoto/ Thinkstock, (3) Dorling Kindersley RF/Thinkstock, (8) David Henderson/iStock Editorial/Thinkstock; **15**: Photodisc/Thinkstock; **17**: iStockphoto/Thinkstock; **19**: (buffet, hiking, skiing, pool party, clubbing) iStockphoto/Thinkstock, (sightseeing) Jupiterimages/ BananaStock/Thinkstock, (hot spring) Photodisc/Thinkstock; **20**: (1) Ingram Publishing/Thinkstock, (2, 4, 5, 7) iStockphoto/ Thinkstock, (3) Fuse/Thinkstock, (6) Stockbyte/Thinkstock, (8) Keith Levit Photography/Thinkstock; **21**: (t) iStockphoto/Thinkstock, (b) Ron Chapple Stock/Thinkstock; **22**: iStockphoto/Thinkstock; **23**: (t) Photodisc/Thinkstock, (b) iStockphoto/Thinkstock; **25**: (t, l to r) Digital Vision, Fuse, Huntstock, iStock/Thinkstock, (m, l to r) iStock, Ingram Publishing/Thinkstock; **26**: iStockphoto/ Thinkstock; **28**: (1) Fuse/Thinkstock, (2-7) iStock/Thinkstock, (8) Digital Vision/Thinkstock; **29**: (t) Digital Vision/Thinkstock, (b) iStockphoto/Thinkstock; **30**: iStockphoto/Thinkstock; **31**: (t) Purestock/Thinkstock, (b) Fuse/Thinkstock; **32-33**: iStockphoto/ Thinkstock; **34**: (1) Design Pics/Thinkstock, (2) Blend Images/Thinkstock, (3) Stockbyte/Thinkstock, (4-8) iStockphoto/Thinkstock; **35-36**: iStockphoto/Thinkstock; **37**: (t, m) iStockphoto/Thinkstock, (b) amana images/Thinkstock; **38**: (t, 1, 2) iStockphoto/Thinkstock, (3) Jupiterimages/Thinkstock, (4) Monkey Business/Thinkstock; **39**: (gym, b) iStockphoto/Thinkstock, (afternoon tea) moodboard/ Thinkstock, (conference) Digital Vision/Thinkstock ; **40**: (1, 2) moodboard/Thinkstock, (3) Ingram Publishing/Thinkstock, (4-7) iStockphoto/Thinkstock, (8) Push/Thinkstock; **41**: (t) Fuse/Thinkstock, (b) iStockphoto/Thinkstock; **42**: (t) iStockphoto/Thinkstock, (b) iStockphoto/Thinkstock; **43**: (t, b) iStockphoto/Thinkstock, (m) Monkey Business/Thinkstock; **44**: (t) iStockphoto/Thinkstock, (b) Wavebreak Media/Thinkstock; **45**: (t, l to r) Hemera, iStockphoto/Thinkstock, (Paul) Fuse/Thinkstock, (Eddie) Photick/Thinkstock, (Mike) iStockphoto/Thinkstock; **46**: iStockphoto/Thinkstock; **48-49**: iStockphoto/Thinkstock; **50**: (t) iStockphoto/Thinkstock, (b) F1online/Thinkstock; **51**: iStockphoto/Thinkstock, (b) Purestock/Thinkstock; **52-53**: iStockphoto/Thinkstock; **54**: (1) Fuse/Thinkstock, (2-7) iStockphoto/Thinkstock, (8) Digital Vision/Thinkstock; **55**: (t) Keith Levit Photography/Thinkstock, (m) Photodisc/Thinkstock, (b) iStockphoto/Thinkstock; **56-58, 60**: iStockphoto/Thinkstock; **61**: (t) Ingram Publishing/Thinkstock, (m) Wavebreak Media/ Thinkstock; **62**: (t) Wavebreak Media/Thinkstock, (b) iStockphoto/Thinkstock; **63**: Photodisc/Thinkstock; **65**: (meeting, giving, visitng) iStockphoto/Thinkstock, (restaurant) Fuse/Thinkstock, (work) Monkey Business/Thinkstock; **66**: iStockphoto/Thinkstock; **68**: (1) Getty Images News/Thinkstock, (2) Zoonar RF/Thinkstock, (3-8) iStockphoto/Thinkstock; **69**: (t, b) iStockphoto/Thinkstock, (m) Getty Images News/Thinkstock; **70**: iStockphoto/Thinkstock; **71**: (t, m) Getty Images News/Thinkstock, (b) iStockphoto/Thinkstock; **72**: (t) Getty Images News/Thinkstock, (b) Creatas/Thinkstock; **73**: iStockphoto/Thinkstock; **74**: (1) Hemera/Thinkstock, (2-8) iStockphoto/Thinkstock; **75**: iStockphoto/Thinkstock; **76**: (t) iStockphoto/Thinkstock, (b) Creatas/Thinkstock; **77**: (t, m) iStockphoto/ Thinkstock, (b) Creatas/Thinkstock; **78**: Digital Vision/Thinkstock; **79**: iStockphoto/Thinkstock; **80**: (m) Hemera/Thinkstock, (8, 9) iStockphoto/Thinkstock, (10) Getty Images News/Thinkstock; **81**: (t, b) iStockphoto/Thinkstock, (m) Digital Vision/Thinkstock; **82**: (t) Purestock/Thinkstock, (m) iStockphoto/Thinkstock; **83**: (t, m) Creatas/Thinkstock, (b) iStockphoto/Thinkstock; **84**: (t) TongRo Images/Thinkstock, (b) iStockphoto/Thinkstock; **85**: iStockphoto/Thinkstock; **86**: Photodisc/Thinkstock; **88**: (1) Purestock/Thinkstock, (2) moodboard/Thinkstock, (3-5, 7) iStockphoto/Thinkstock, (6) iStock Editorial/Thinkstock, (8) Digital Vision/Thinkstock; **89**: (t, b) iStockphoto/Thinkstock, (m) Photodisc/Thinkstock; **90**: iStockphoto/Thinkstock; **91**: (t, m) iStockphoto/Thinkstock, (b) Fuse/Thinkstock; **92-93**: iStockphoto/Thinkstock; **94**: (1) Tetra Images/Thinkstock, (2-7) Tetra Images/Thinkstock, (8) Photodisc/ Thinkstock; **95**: (t) Digital Vision/Thinkstock, (m) Zoonar/Thinkstock, (b) Pixland/Thinkstock; **96**: iStockphoto/Thinkstock; **97**: (t) F1online/Thinkstock, (m) iStockphoto/Thinkstock; **98**: (t) Digital Vision/Thinkstock, (m) moodboard/Thinkstock; **99**: iStockphoto/ Thinkstock; **100-101**: iStockphoto/Thinkstock; **102**: Digital Vision/Thinkstock; **103**: (t, m) iStockphoto/Thinkstock, (b) Creatas/ Thinkstock; **104**: iStockphoto/Thinkstock; **105**: (New York) Photodisc/Thinkstock, (London, Paris, Rome, Berlin) iStockphoto/ Thinkstock, (Barcelona) Top Photo Group/Thinkstock, (b, l to r) iStockphoto, Fuse/Thinkstock; **106**: iStockphoto/Thinkstock.